Chain Reaction
Children and Divorce

Ofra Ayalon and Adina Flasher

Jessica Kingsley Publishers
London and Bristol, Pennsylvania

The authors and the publishers gratefully acknowledge permission to reprint the following:

The extract from *Motherhood: The Second Oldest Profession* (1983) by Erma Bombeck, is reprinted by permission of The Aaron M. Priest Literary Agency.

The extracts from *Offerit Blofferit* by Ehud Ben-Ezer (1979) are reprinted by the kind permission of the author.

The extracts from *The Soul Bird* by Michal Snunit (1984) are reprinted by permission of the Massada Publishers.

The extract from *Zebra Zebroni* by Oded Burla (1986) is reprinted by the kind permission of the author.

The verses by Shlomo Raviv are printed by the kind permission of the author.

The extracts from *Peoplemaking* by Virginia Satir (1972) are reprinted by kind permission of **the author.**

Based on the Hebrew book *On Children and Divorce*, published in 1987 by Nord Publications, Israel.

First published in English in the United Kingdom in 1993 by
Jessica Kingsley Publishers Ltd
116 Pentonville Road
London N1 9JB

Copyright © 1993 Ofra Ayalon and Adina Flasher

British Library Cataloguing in Publication Data

Ayalon, Ofra
Chain Reaction: Children and Divorce
I. Title II. Flasher, Adina
362.7

ISBN 1 85302 136 9

Printed and Bound in Great Britain by
Biddles Ltd., Guildford and King's Lynn

Dedication

In memory of our parents

'perhaps love is the process of my
leading you gently back to yourself'

Acknowledgements

Our deep thanks go to the many children who trusted us and opened windows to their souls. We know that your new, inner self-discovery as well as your new understanding of the grown-up world will help you.

Our own children, as always, have taught us most about the world of children and have kept the fountainhead of our love flowing.

Our book represents a blending of talents and efforts of many people:

Alida Gersie, our exquisite and unique friend, who has been a source of inspiration and a guide into the world of charming stories and original structures.

Dr Mooli Lahad, with gratitude and admiration. Your coping and survival against all odds has taught us the greatest lesson of 'mind over matter' and the power or love to regenerate life.

Melanie Hoffstad, for your richness of spirit, your creativity, your sensitivity and for the experience of connecting the mind and the body.

Yael Avraham. For being there.

Geula Grossman. For your contribution to the lucidity and fluency of the text.

Tzvi Remetz, our graphic artist, thank you for your lively illustrations.

Jessica Kingsley and **Helen Skelton**, thank you for your trust and endless patience, and for providing a secure atmosphere in which our book could grow and mature.

It is difficult to mention everyone by name, but we wish to thank various divorce experts, authors and friends, as well as our university and college students, divorced parents, teachers and counsellors who have contributed valuable feedback. Special thanks go to **Ziva Falk**, the headmistress who believes in our work and opens all the doors to our children.

Last but not least, love and thanks to our partners, **Arodi** and **Israel.**

Contents

Part II: A Helping Hand

Part III Mind Over Matter

Part IV: Support Groups for Children

Part V: The Child and the Family

Introduction

The fact that divorced, blended and one-parent families have become a prevalent phenomena in our culture and are no longer associated with the stigma of social or psychological pathology has not blinded us to the plight of children. Divorce extracts a high price by causing a massive amount of stress. Children of all ages, and from the most privileged as well as underprivileged families, are susceptible to its consequences.

According to recent estimates at least a million children experience parental divorce annually in the United States. In other Western countries, such as the United Kingdom and Israel, the numbers are growing. One out of every three children under the age of eighteen has experienced divorce. The stressful nature of that experience increases the likelihood of adverse effects on the children's psychological well-being.

Divorce is a longitudinal process in the life of children and their parents that begins long before the actual breakup, and continues long after it. As the family system undergoes various forms of crises, children often develop feelings of alienation, anger, confusion and despair. If there is no intervention during the various stages of divorce, there are identifiable consequences for the child's development. Numerous studies report detrimental cognitive, behavioural and psychophysiological effects on many children of divorce.

The divorce itself leads to the disintegration of the family nucleus. This 'nuclear reaction' releases destructive energies. With suitable guidance, it is possible to channel these energies in a constructive way towards the building of new family structures, such as binuclear family systems. A great deal of support, professional help and intervention is needed to help the family adapt to the new binuclear family structure.

Our book is designed to help families move safely through the dangerous curves of the maze of divorce. Many years of touching children's lives in our therapeutic work have convinced us that our approach is conducive to seeing children overcome disastrous life-events. It suggests a sensible approach focused on the direct experience of the child and the verbal and non-verbal expression of this experience, awareness, insight and control.

In order to address a large variety of coping styles we suggest a rich menu of strategies: physical activities and relaxation; emotional expression of the full range of feelings; cognitive methods of problem-solving, self-control and internal dialogues, values clarification and positive thinking. The main vehicles of this approach are stories and metaphors which trigger curiosity, humour, intuition and creativity. All methods are adaptable towards individual, family, and group activities. We help shared-fate groups to develop into most helpful support systems.

This book is meant to be a guide for parents, relatives, teachers and therapists to help them find a safe path in the unchartered territory of the life of divorce. It is dedicated to the children who have to tread this path.

PART ONE

THE MAZE OF DIVORCE

CHAPTER ONE

Parenthood on the Line

Life After Divorce

The act of divorce may turn into 'a time bomb' that threatens the psychological welfare of both the parents and children. To reduce and control this danger, it is essential to change the pathology and stigma of failure attached to it. Divorce may best be seen as a series of life-cycle passages, in which a faulty system develops into a new set of more satisfactory relationships for the parents in which the children can also find their place. Coping with divorce requires both deep understanding and insight into the causes of the dissolution of the family unit, as well as an active search for new patterns of parenthood.

The numerous changes following divorce cause a 'chain reaction'. Changes in lifestyle – whether expected or unexpected, good or bad – are powerful stressors, upsetting the existing balance and demanding reorganisation. These stressors are potentially very dangerous to the psychological and the physical well-being of everyone involved. The more one is exposed to stresses and the longer their duration, the greater is the danger (Selye 1966).

In the *aftermath* of divorce, two different manifestations of stress evolve: the acute crisis and the chronic state. Stress reaches its peak with the onset of simultaneous or rapidly successive changes, usually beginning with the signing of the divorce papers. However, the overthrow of the precarious balance of the family unit, which began long before this stage, does not end with the divorce. In the course of 'life after divorce', a great deal of tension accumulates and develops into highly dangerous states of chronic stress. These may lower thresholds of resistance to mental and physical diseases and severely reduce both parents' and children's ability to cope. Just as a handful of pebbles thrown into a pool creates endless ripples, so does parental separation. These ripples are both concentric and colliding.

The family break-up affects many levels of function and behaviour, and poses new demands at each level (Ware 1983). These levels appear in varying orders and with varying degrees of difficulty, but all of them exacerbate the on-going crisis:

- *The legal level.* Revocation of the marriage contract and application to the courts for a legal separation.

- *The economic level.* Division of the joint economic unit into two independent ones. Often, the units retain some economic interdependence in the form of alimony, child support, joint responsibilities in business and joint property being kept for the children.

- *The physical level.* The family moves into two separate dwellings. The geographical distance between them is undetermined.

- *The sexual level.* Ending the physical and sexual intimacy between ex-spouses.

- *The emotional level.* After the separation there is no interparental moral and emotional support; on the contrary, open or covert hostility is very often present.

- *The role level.* Relinquishment of roles in the family, such as 'wife', 'husband'; the severance of family relationships with in-laws and other relatives.

- *The social level.* Acceptance of the new 'single' status, socially and legally, and making contact with other single parents.

- *The parental level.* The ex-couple must learn to concentrate on the needs of the child and separate them from their own. At the very least they must reach an agreement on co-operation as parents in the best interests of the children, despite the anger, hostility and alienation that exist on various planes.

At each of these levels, each family member adapts at his or her own pace and with different degrees of involvement. Stress brought on by divorce emanates from the experience of loss and change. The influence of these experiences varies according to the individual. Kanner, Coyne, Schafer and Lazarus (1981) found a high degree of physical and psychological damage caused by these stressful experiences. Holmes and Raye (1967) provided us with a scale to measure the deleterious effects of accumulated stress. The highest score, 100, is assigned to the stress caused by the death of a spouse. Divorce, which is very close to 'death' on this scale, receives 73 points. However, this score is misleading, as it does not take into account the changes brought about by divorce, each one of which has its own score. If we add only a few of the changes resulting from divorce, we obtain the following scores:

Change in the economic situation	38
Change in the number of quarrels in the family	35
Change in personal habits	24
Change of living conditions	20
Change in patterns of leisure	19
Change in sleeping habits	16
Change in number of family get-togethers	15

Thus, the total score produced by powerful divorce-related stressors often approaches 258, nearing the danger line of 300, which signifies total collapse.

These measures of stress were determined for adults: the scale of measurement for children would presumably be different as it would reflect the centrality of various aspects of divorce in their lives. Although children are more flexible and open to change, their dependence on their parents makes them very vulnerable to the turbulence in the latter's lives. To develop normally, children need consistency and security in their relationships with their parents. Young children experience the events surrounding them through the mediation of the adults close to them. Like a seismograph, children absorb the finest of tremors in family stability and react to any disruption of the balance of family life.

Disputes Over Children

Major decisions determining the fate of the children are taken when the divorce crisis is at its peak. In all respects, this is the worst possible timing, as the ability to make decisions is distorted under stress (Wheeler and Janis 1980). It is therefore not surprising that many problems concerning the daily lives of the children are left unsolved as the stress surrounding the upheaval in parental roles makes it almost impossible to work out the details of the new relationships. The separating parents reach the numerous decisions concerning their children in one of three ways:

- by mutual consent
- by bargaining or coercion
- through the intervention of an objective outsider.

The dissolution of the family can deprive the parents of much of their authority over their children: if there is no mutual agreement, the final decisions concerning their children's welfare will be made by the courts.

In court, the parents often appear as enemies. It is amazing and alarming to see parents competing over the custody of their children and investing economic and emotional resources in the fight over them – often more than they invested in their mutual care for them.

Too little guidance is given to the divorcing parents in this difficult period of their lives. The court decides parental rights and duties in very general terms, so that they will be accepted by both sides, and the lawyers who prepare the settlement do not tend to bring the dilemmas likely to occur later to their clients' attention. Nor do they offer any solutions to the emerging problems, although it is precisely these difficulties that need to be aired before the divorce settlement.

Later quarrels or misunderstandings tend to threaten or distort previously reached agreements and to endanger the relative security achieved in the children's lives. Parental success or failure to reach agreement influences their children's daily lives not only in the present, but also far into the future, shaping their attitudes towards marriage, family life and parental responsibility when they themselves reach maturity.

> 'I shall never marry,' declares a girl of 12. 'I don't want to have children who will have to suffer the way we did when our parents divorced.'

In conditions of uncertainty and unexpected changes in parental lives and attitudes, it is clear that the judicial system is incapable of producing any set laws covering the vast number of daily problems. By default, therefore, the responsibilities of decision-making are usually left to the parents.

When the marriage is dissolved, the parents are faced with fateful decisions concerning the divided parental role and the rebuilding of completely new parental patterns. In the present system, one parent receives custody of the children, and thus establishes him- or herself as the permanent or central parent in a one-parent family. The other becomes the peripheral 'accidental' parent – the one who comes to visit and is called, sometimes sarcastically and sometimes with pain, 'the weekend parent'. In some instances, this parent withdraws completely, keeping out of sight and becoming an 'ex-parent'.

The court determines custody according to what is 'for the child's own good'. How is this judged? How is it possible to choose between parents, when both seem suitable and each one is certain that the child's own good demands that he or she be the only custodial parent?

During the custody battle, when angers are at their peak, hidden motives totally unconnected to the children's welfare surface. Gardner (1976) asserts that custody wars have many causes, and not all of them concern the child's best interests. Custody may be a bargaining tool in the conflict over alimony and support payments. Any arrangement which can save money is often preferred. The family home often reverts to the custodial parent. Vengeance is an additional motive in the fight over custody. The best way to hurt the partner is by taking the children away from her or him. An American jurist described a father's fight for custody over his two sons. After he had won the case, he returned the children to their mother, saying 'I just wanted you to know that I could beat you' (Wheeler 1980).

In the battle of wits and revenge, one parent may be prepared to slander the other, laying all sorts of accusations and failures at his or her door, so as to subvert the law and legally 'kidnap' the children. The child may be seen as a reward, a symbol of the 'victorious' parent's rectitude.

Divorce Mediation

Because of the difficulties involved in making parenting decisions, new types of guidance and counselling are needed. Divorce counselling has two main goals. First, each partner should be given the kind of support which reduces bitterness, diminishes feelings of victimisation, and accentuates the positive aspects or conflict resolution. Second, counselling should facilitate bargaining, enabling the parents to reach a mutually acceptable legal agreement structuring the discontinuation of the marital relationship and defining their new parental roles. This assignment is very difficult to achieve in the given crisis situation. It calls for innovative counselling methods which will:

- develop methods of communication between the parents, either directly or through with the help of a third party
- help parents reach agreement on the principles and practices concerning their children
- open a channel for revising old decisions in the light of new developments
- determine in advance acceptable ways of setting disagreements (compromise, arbitration, and so on).

To satisfy this need, a new approach, known as divorce mediation, has recently been developed. Divorce mediation tries to help the couple reach mutually acceptable solutions. Mediation addresses the psychological needs of the family as a whole and of its individual members, as well as the legal aspects of the divorce agreement. It deals with three main areas:

1. The division of property accumulated by the couple during their life together, taking into account that both have the right to a fair settlement.

2. Supporting the ending of mutual dependence and achieving emotional separation.

3. The encouragement of parental co-operation in bringing up their children.

The mediator needs to solicit the estranged parents' cooperation. The choice of mediation demands the active participation of both partners and their understanding that a compromise does not mean losing. A neutral mediator, acting according to rules and procedures decided in advance, may help the couple escape the whirlpool of emotional stress that distorts their capacity to make fair and sensible decisions. Three ground-rules are recommended:

1. Non-adversarial discussions.

2. Mutuality in decision-making and agreement over performance.

3. Leaving control over the decisions to the parents.

Unfortunately, mediation begins at the worst psychological moment, when both partners are immersed in stormy emotional upheavals of anger, grief, jealousy, hatred and revenge. Destructive behaviour, characterised by 'unfinished business', is likely to disrupt the course of mediation. Anger that has not been relieved or mitigated during divorce may increase after separation and nullify the achievement of mediation. The counsellor has to identify and minimise behaviours which can sabotage the mediation process, and to help the divorcing couple conceptualise and formulate their post-separation relationship.

Mediation is carried out by a therapist (for example, a psychologist, psychiatrist or social worker), and the contract is drawn up by a lawyer who represents both sides. The mediator, exercising skills of negotiation management and conflict resolution (Zaidel 1991), serves the whole family's interests, especially protecting those of the children.

In the divorce struggle, children may become hostages. Very often they are perceived as property:

They belong to me.

I've invested everything in them.

They are my security for the future.

Sometimes children are used as pawns for gaining rights and bonuses:

If you don't pay up, you won't see the children.

In the end the children are the ones who pay the highest emotional price. Ruth, aged fifteen, expressed the feelings of many children of divorced parents:

I'm sorry I was born. Because of me, my parents have been quarreling for ten years. If I weren't here, maybe they would have stopped.

A study of adolescents who attempted suicide found among them a great number of children of divorce, whose parents had continued fighting at their expense many years after the separation (Cohen 1985). Divorce mediation has a potential for preventing this damaging effect. Through mediation, the parents learn to deal openly and directly with the emotional aspects of the separation and refrain from using their children for personal or financial gain. Parents learn to see their children as people in their own right, with needs and feelings of their own (Haynes 1981). The mediator prevents escalation of tension, helps the couple escape past entanglements, and prepares them for possible future scenarios. The mediator uses the knowledge of children's needs in the various developmental stages and behaviour under crisis to decipher their distress signals as calls for help. The mediator passes this understanding on to the parents, to prevent them from wrongly interpreting children's symptoms.

Following divorce, many children express fears of being abandoned. They may make desperate attempts to reunite their parents and use extreme methods to win the parents' attention, test or punish them. These distress signals may be interpreted differently by each of the parents, and the battles between them are fueled by these different interpretations. The mediator's task is to define the children's needs without becoming involved in their provocative behaviour. Consider the following example:

> Dan, aged three, wets his bed and bursts out crying every time he returns from a visit to his father's.
>
> *The mother's interpretation:* The visits to his father have a very bad influence on the child.
>
> *The father's interpretation:* The child prefers staying with his father and refuses to return to the mother.

This is an opportunity for the mediator to translate the child's behaviour to his parents, explaining that bedwetting is the child's way of expressing fears of abandonment and worries about survival; in addition, the hidden purpose may be to reunite his father and mother. Once the parents understand, they may respond more aptly to the child's needs, instead of arguing over him.

Very young children have a limited understanding of what is happening around them. They unwittingly exacerbate misunderstanding between the parents because each parent interprets the child's behaviour according to his or her own needs and motives. Asking children to be reasonable when their world is collapsing is an impossible demand. Laura's story is a very vivid example:

> Laura, four years old, tells her father during her visit with him that her mother hasn't been bringing any food home lately. 'Would you come over to us this evening and bring us some oranges and cocoa?' In this way the girl expressed her fear that her mother might also leave her. She tries to revive her sense of security by making her father feed her. The father, who takes this as proof that the mother is not bringing up the child properly, demands that the girl be given over to his sole custody. The mother also sues for sole custody of the girl, stating that the father is spoiling her.

The parents may be trapped by their own uncontrollable feelings. There are fathers who insist on having their children fifty per cent of the time, in spite of the inconvenience this causes everyone involved, including the fathers themselves! This demand probably derives from a sense of vengeance and a wish to prove who is in control. Another example is the mother, bitter over the father's rigid interpretation of the custody ruling, who demands exclusive custody of the children. Without intervention, this struggle between the parents may escalate, frightening the children even more and increasing the parent's rigidity, imprisoning them all within a vicious cycle.

Children can gain a lot from participating in the mediation process. The mediator represents the child and brings his or her viewpoint before both parents. Thus, children regain some sense of control over their lives, even though the divorce is forced upon them. Including the children in the mediation process allows them to hear, be heard, and develop a perspective about the difficult situation into which they have been forced. Most of the children leave mediation sessions with feelings of relief and with a deeper understanding of the complications surrounding the divorce situation. The parents gain a deeper understanding of the unnecessary agony that their perpetual competitiveness inflicts on their children. This understanding helps the parents to concentrate on their children's needs and to try to minimise their suffering.

Split Custody

> And the king said: Fetch me a sword. And they brought a sword before the king. And the king said: Divide the living child in two, and give half to the one, and half to the other.
>
> (*I Kings* 3:23-25)

In an intact family, the maxim 'fathers are parents too' is often used as a challenge for fathers to actively participate in the upbringing of their children. In divorce trials, however, this statement can escalate custody battles. The stereotyped perception that only the mother is capable of nurturing young children is changing, with many fathers demanding the right to bring up their children, declaring that 'it has not been proved that the ability to look after, nurture, feed and love the child is a genetic characteristic bestowed by nature to the female sex only' (Ayalon 1983).

There are marked differences of opinion among psychologists over what is best for the welfare of the child. Numerous researchers believe that the child needs one 'psychological parent' to supply him or her with stability and constancy (Goldstein, Freud and Solnit 1973). According to this approach, children of divorced parents do not require two parental figures, but for their own good, they should have one positive model for identification. It recommends dividing parenthood, thereby freeing the child of the need for double loyalties. Other researchers (Wallerstein and Kelly 1980) have reached antithetical conclusions: children who have not had a constant and frequent relationship with both parents have been found to suffer from very low self-esteem.

In deciding the consequences of divided parenthood, not only is the gender of the custodial parent considered, but also the parent's lifestyle. In a divorce, the decision over the family lifestyle appropriate for the child is transferred from the parents to the judge, who hands over exclusive custody of the child to one of the parents. The decisive, value-oriented decisions, therefore, now rest with the judge. For example, what is best for the child?

- To live with the father in economic security or to be given the opportunity of developing intellectual and artistic talents with the mother?

- To receive strict religious education at the mother's home or a liberal education at the father's?

- To be exposed to the various stimuli of city life or to live close to nature in the country?

When parents fight over custody, all their customs, beliefs, work styles and social habits are on trial. But there are no social norms that enable the judge to classify, categorise, or give marks for different lifestyles. When the child is given over to the custody of one of the parents, that parent becomes the sole authority deciding the mode of the child's life and his or her standard of living. We must realise that each of the proposed solutions has its own risk factors.

Children growing up in one-parent families develop early, learn to organise their life without much support and take on responsibilities. Reality dictates that they help with housework and look after themselves, which in itself contributes to growing up. However, whereas children's cooperation in the upkeep of the household and taking care of themselves is considered very desirable, the inability to differentiate between parental and child roles may cause trouble for both parent and child. It can often reduce the child's developmental space and impede the parent's (most often the mother's) ability to rehabilitate her or his social life. By sharing household-management responsibilities with her children, the mother risks losing her rights as an adult, and the children may lose the authoritative figure they so desperately need. The supporting figure in their lives, whose task it is to lay a good foundation for their security with clear and consistent boundaries, becomes incapable of doing just that.

More subtle dangers lurking in the one-parent family system derive from the symbolic values parents attach to children. The child may symbolise the failure of the marriage, or be a perpetual reminder of the parent who has left. Sometimes the child is perceived as an economic burden or as a disturbance to the freshly developing intimacy with a new partner. As a result, rejection of the child may develop. The 'catch' in the one-parent family is sometimes over-compensation, cloaking feelings of guilt towards the child.

Children can be also active in instigating conflicts. They can become nuisances by manipulating quarries and disturbing new relationships.

> When I come home mad
> From dad,
> I hiss at the cat,
> Kick the mat,
> And don't even want to
> Talk to mother.

All he says then,
My dad, is:
    It's YOUR imagination,
    YOUR imagination.
    I'm sorry I'm late,
    But I have to state
    That with ME he's never
    A bother.

(S. Raviv)

Trapped in the One-Parent System

As a system, the family changes with every addition or loss of a member. A one-parent family is not simply an ordinary one with a missing parent. It is a system different in structure and dynamics. In the two-parent family there are separate boundaries for the parents and for the children. The rules and regulations and the vital decisions are made by the adults. In the majority of cases, the parents support each other in conflict resolution and the solving of problems. Roles such as decision making, erotic and sexual satisfaction, social interests, economic cooperation and problem-solving are assumed together or alternately. While the parents in an intact family are involved in their mutual relationship, the children are free to fulfil age-appropriate goals and interact with peers. The parental sub-system is a cradle of security and emotional nurturing (Minuchin 1974). In an intact family, there is a greater probability that one of the parents will always be available to attend to the physical and emotional needs of the child.

The new family nucleus formed after a divorce differs from the former family structure mainly in that it replaces the patterns of mutuality and cooperation of the two-parent family with the one-way responsibility of the single adult. The child is often expected to take on the role of the missing partner, to support the remaining parent and to assume tasks not suited to his or her age.

The equilibrium of the system can easily be upset and the children may become the tone- setters at home. Such exchange of roles is detected, for example, when the child sleeps in the mother's bed or becomes her confidante, helps her with social problems and decision-making, undertakes the responsibility of caring for younger siblings, or interferes in her relationships with men.

Early, at dawn,
You shoo out your friends,
Who tiptoe out of the house
I know, somehow, you must be shy,
But let me, at least, say good-bye!!

(S. Raviv)

The 'Other' Parent

The visiting parent may try to develop exaggerated means for preserving the connection with his or her child, such as concentrated attention, unusual outings, presents and promises. As a result, an unrealistic relationship develops, casting the visiting parent in the 'angel' role and the custodial parent – the one who is constantly present, feeds, educates, and makes demands – in the 'demon' role.

It is also possible that the parent who has left is not interested in the child and is trying to erase the past. In this case, the child is often frustrated and may suffer badly from damaged self-esteem. In other cases, the abandoning parent, suffering from guilt feelings, may vacillate between bouts of spoiling or ignoring the child. This confuses and frustrates the child, who has no way of knowing or understanding the 'other' parent's true feelings.

Sometimes children are not so eager to meet the visiting parent. They are engrossed in social activities and may experience the visits as a burden. As the children grow up, the prearranged visits may clash with their own plans. A lot of blame, grief and anger arises between parents who demand the right to visit, and children who prefer to spend the time with their peers. Playgrounds and amusement parks are the backdrop for meetings between an uptight father and a bored son or daughter, who are going through the motions of spending the allotted time of the weekly visit.

The estrangement between parents and child may assume features of emotional abuse and neglect. Lack of sensitivity to the child's needs is shown in the following story.

> After my father left us, he never took any interest in me or my mother. He was very preoccupied with his business and was always meeting important business associates to whom he wanted to show me off. The insufficient alimony, which was never enough to sustain us, was paid with extreme precision, but he always refused any special request. I once needed a new pair of shoes very badly, but he refused to buy them for me, saying it was not his duty to do so. That very same day he took me to an exclusive restaurant, where I almost choked on the expensive meal, which cost more than three pairs of shoes.

CHAPTER TWO

Children as Pawns

Painful Games

Each of the former partners, whether living alone, with the children, with parents or with a new partner creates a new family system. In these new systems, the children who have survived the divorce are often deprived of their place. When the rivalry between the divorced parents persists, their children may be used as pawns. The three most common patterns of using and abusing children are described below as: 'blocking', 'tossing', and 'splitting' (Ayalon 1983).

Blocking

This pattern is created by parents who have completely broken off relations with each other. The custodial parent may exclude the other totally, blocking his or her access to the family. Such hostile severance is often a disguise for deep

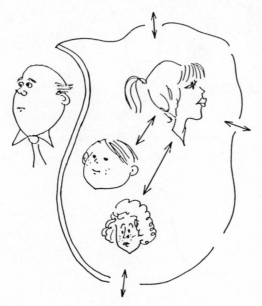

Figure 2.1: Blocking

involvement that has not yet dissipated and is still replete with negative emotions and feelings.

An extreme example is Erica's case: To prevent her children's father from having any relationship with them, Erica left the country without warning immediately after the divorce, leaving no address. She told her children that their father wanted nothing to do with them and described him as a negative and dangerous person. The father invested much time and money searching for his children and two years later found their hiding place. He tried to contact them, but they were terrified of him, even refusing to talk to him on the phone. The mother managed to produce a court order against his entering their home.

Tossing

In many cases the child is tossed from one parent to the other. Parents, exploiting their children's passages back and forth between households, make them 'carrier pigeons' for nasty messages or various demands. Children suffer badly when they are used in this tug of war. Amanda, aged five, describing her dream, expressed her feelings of being torn between her parents:

> I dreamed I was a train chained to two engines, and each engine was pulling in the opposite direction...

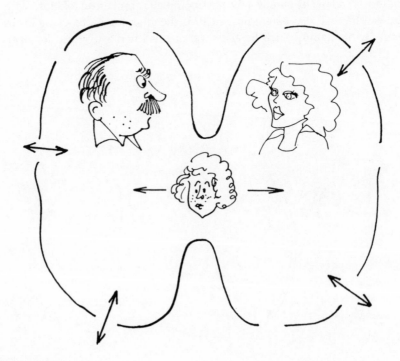

Figure 2.2: Tossing

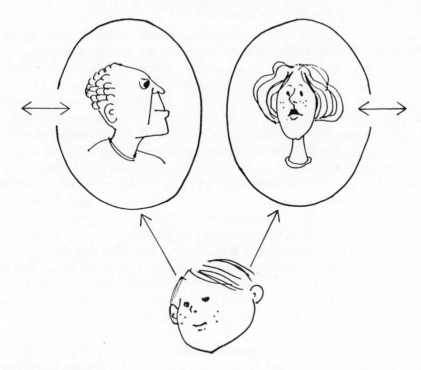

Figure 2.3: Splitting

Splitting

There is no custody arrangement that guarantees parental or children's happiness. Some parents are only interested in holding equal rights, but do not arrange the necessary conditions of living in permanent and geographically close residences; some doubt the ability of the other parent to bring up the child properly and cannot reach a mutual understanding; others project different norms and values concerning daily living and attitudes to life. The child's exposure to two different family systems can be quite confusing. Without psychological continuity, the transitions between the two lifestyles may be disruptive for the child.

Custody must not be allowed to turn into a sort of 'Solomon's trial', where the child is cut into two. Parents in competition may decide to share custody, and then, upon discovering that they are unable to carry it out, demand that the child be sent to an institution or boarding school: 'If I can't have her, neither can you!'

Sharing Custody: The Bi-Nuclear Family

In this *modus vivendi*, the father and the mother create two separate families with permeable boundaries. The children can move between them without any difficulty. Both parents have completed the process of separation and have begun the process of rebuilding their independent lives. In a bi-nuclear arrangement, children find their places in two family systems, that of the mother and that of the father. They can divide the days of the week between them, decide to switch from one home to the other every month or, if preferred, live for half a year at each parent's home. If the geographical distance does not allow this, the year may be divided into school time and holidays. The child stays with one parent when at school but spends holidays with the other. The aim of shared custody is to prevent the child from experiencing the feeling of loss that accompanies the parents' divorce, as well as utilising the advantages of maximum involvement and firm contacts with both parents. The chief advantage for children is that their upbringing is in the hands of both parents and they do not have to choose between them. The danger of split loyalty is also reduced. Shared custody reduces the parents' burden concerning the child's upbringing, which is especially important in times of stress, such as when one of the parents is sick. Shared custody prevents ugly courtroom custody battles and cumulative feelings of bitterness.

Even in the potentially benign case of shared custody, it is still necessary to help the child cope with the disturbing effects of perpetually shifting from one home to another. The hassle of moving back and forth is compensated for by the promise of love and continuity of contact with both parents.

Figure 2.4: Sharing

Shared Custody, as Seen by Children

> Sleeping one night on the closed balcony at mother's and the next night on the couch in my father's living-room.

> Having a bath at my father's and taking a shower at my mother's.

> It's sausage sandwiches for lunch at my father's and vegetarian health food at my mother's.

> On Tuesdays I do my maths lessons with my father, and my history homework with my mother every Thursday.

> My problem is that my running shoes are always left behind at my mother's when I sleep at my father's, and at my father's when I sleep at my mother's!

> When I invite friends over to my house, I always have to explain whether by 'my house' I mean at my mother's or my father's.

In shared custody, it is of paramount importance that the home of each of the divorced parents should also be the home of the child.

Two homes for one child? Isn't this arrangement rather confusing and embarrassing? Studies show (Ricci 1980) that children's adaptation improves the more they feel wanted in their parents' homes. Children adapt easily to various sources of authority. In the family, on the street, at school, in extra curricular activities, children are capable of adjusting to different rules. The child's full membership in the two families created through the parents' divorce is the best proof that they have divorced from each other but have not separated from their children. Both father and mother commit themselves to continue individually what they previously undertook together: bringing up their children. Each parent can develop her or his own personal style and educational methods which may differ from the other's without opposing or undermining it. The separated parents do not divide the *children* between them, only the amount of time the child spends with each.

Creating two intact but separate homes without lapsing into fighting is a lengthy process. The parents learn to distinguish between the idea of the family and the idea of marriage. Marriage does start the family, but divorce does not end it. Even after a marriage is over, the family does not disappear but changes, dividing into two. The pattern of two homes also promotes stability in the new lives of the parents, thus leading to stability in the lives of their children.

It is important to observe a few rules to ease adaptation to this complex way of life. The feeling of belonging to two homes is reinforced when the child does not have to carry suitcases from place to place, even if the time spent in one of them is short. The feeling of belonging, not the amount of time spent in each house, is the decisive factor. The children need their own space, even if it is only a drawer, some toiletries, clothes, toys and some concrete proof, such as permanent sleeping arrangements, to ensure their belonging to the home.

In the first stages of becoming acquainted with the parent's new home, it is worth investing time in exploring the new surroundings together, meeting neighbours and potential friends, and deciding on safety rules and the extent of the child's freedom to wander alone. This is also an opportunity to determine rules of behaviour and division of roles between the two parents.

The Advantages of the 'Two Homes' Approach

- Direct parental relationships with the children. Establishing a new parental identity after losing (or relinquishing) the former role as a partner and a married parent.
- Parents maintain direct relationships with the other adults in their children's lives, such as teachers, doctors and others.
- Sparing the child exposure to continuous fighting between parents.
- Strengthening each former spouse's parental authenticity, in both the children's view and society's.

The main beneficiaries are the children, who gain both security and continued contact with both of their parents.

A Working Relationship Between Divorced Parents

Sharing Time With the Children

A heavy blow to the child's confidence is the feeling that the parents consider the time spent with him or her time wasted. Instead, the parent might see this as an opportunity for strengthening ties with the child. Under no circumstances should the feelings of anger towards the other parent influence attitudes towards the children. However, it is necessary to come to terms with the separation of parental roles. It is not usually worth trying to consult the other parent on special problems or on how to bring up the child. Professional counselling is more advisable.

Territory, Independence and Autonomy

When the child lives with one parent, all the responsibilities and decisions about the child education rest with that parent. When the child lives with the other parent all these decisions become his or hers. Limitations are placed on either parent's autonomy only in the event of danger or abuse to the child (Ricci 1980). Each parent has full rights: it is not fair to make plans that infringe on the other parent's time with the child – this is the principle of non- interference. The children find out what they can expect from each parent separately and are thus saved from the temptation of exploiting conflicting parental beliefs and attaining favours through emotional extortion. Child-power through manipulation is a frightening and harmful substitute for parental responsibility.

The Interparental Relationship

Are messages between parents delivered direct – either in writing or verbally? Or is there indirect communication? Through whom is it delivered? The child? Friends? Lawyers? Does the information concerning the child come direct from the other parent, or is it received through other channels? Is the information reliable? Can it be verified? Is it easy or difficult to get an answer from the other parent?

Parents may be able to utilise their knowledge of the other to plan the most efficient way of eliciting his or her agreement to suggestions. It is advisable for each parent to assess her or his own methods of angering the other parent. When and to what extent are these methods used? How do behaviours evoke negative reactions from the other parent? Can these reactions be changed?

The following rules are recommended for the working relationship between the two parents.

1. It is important to control expressions of feelings. Do not mix feelings with daily arrangements. Even though cool relations do not seem appropriate between people who were once very close, they are now a condition for negotiations over the children.

2. To ensure a calm, regulated and reliable lifestyle, sound and consistent plans should be laid down in writing. It is imperative to keep to timetables, carry out decisions, and plan ahead, taking all eventualities into account and discussing all matters calmly. Avoid bringing up past mistakes and avoid making them in the future!

3. Clarify every problem clearly and avoid assumptions and suppositions before checking. Writing things down helps to clear up confusions. Each parent should have a copy of the written document which both have approved.

4. Do not take the other parent for granted. This approach is both insulting and dangerous.

5. Write notes. Many find this method irritating, but it is also very efficient. When one is awash with stormy feelings, one is apt to forget or distort facts. Some people tend to make general promises without defining the details of the procedures to be used. Writing memos prevents ambiguity and minimises mistaken interpretation of the other parent's statements.

Parents who deal with facts are a boon for their offspring. They prevent the misery and fear that fighting arouses, and show their children how to resolve disagreements without hurting and humiliating each other and without compromising self-respect.

CHAPTER THREE

Through the Child's Eyes

Counting Losses

Divorce may offer adults some benefits, such as a relief from tension, a doorway to freedom or a chance to find a more suitable partner. Children, however, have a lot to lose and very little to gain. Let us examine some losses and gains that divorce holds for children, as reflected in questions that worry many divorced parents:

- Will our divorce cause the child irrevocable emotional damage?
- What measure of natural resilience do children have for withstanding the shocks in the family structure?
- How can we inoculate children against the stress and strains caused by the dissolution of their family, and improve their coping ability?

Divorce involves many changes. Simultaneous occurrence of these changes at a time when the family support system is weakened may increase children's vulnerability.

A number of factors combine to bring about an escalation of the stress level:

Uncertainty About What Is Happening

Many parents keep their decision to divorce secret from their children for a long time. Others tell half-truths in the hope of sparing their children, unaware that they are actually causing them confusion and bewilderment.

Lack of Control Over Their Lives and Over the Family Situation

Divorcing parents often involve their children in struggles over custody, economic support or visiting rights, while children feel totally powerless to stop these struggles. Lack of control generates helplessness, pessimism and depression.

Loss of Parental Support

Caught up in the crisis, parents are so embroiled in their own problems that they barely notice their children's needs. Following the divorce, there are crucial changes in the relationships between children and parents. One of the parents is usually distant or disappears from their life completely, while the custodial parent has to cope with numerous new demands. As a result, the children are often neglected. In many instances, parent–child roles are reversed and the children are expected to care for their parents. In either case they are left with inadequate support.

Divided Loyalties

Children are often caught in the cross-fire between their parent's conflicting demands. The struggle with divided loyalties causes the child direct damage (Hetherington 1979). The criticism and scorn which parents heap on each other devalue them both in the child's eyes, invalidating their authority and disrupting the child's ability to identify with either parent.

Limited Role-Models

In a one-parent family, the missing parent's role leaves a permanent vacuum. The absence of a father or a mother from day-to-day life may deprive the child of security, authority and discipline. The missing parent cannot contribute to the solution of learning and social problems or participate in mutual interests. In addition, distancing a girl or boy from the parent of the opposite sex impedes the development of her or his sexual identification (Santrock and Warshak 1979).

Decline in Economic Welfare

This results from the division of income and property and the limited earning ability of the custodial parent.

Loss of Social Status

The parents' divorce usually leads to children's loss of social status. Because they are 'different' or appear to lack defenders, they often turn into scapegoats within their peer group. Social ostracism may frequently be endorsed by teachers who discriminate against children of divorce because of prejudice and preconceived ideas (Smilansky and Wiessman 1981).

Scholastic Underachievement

Stress, confusion or uncertainty, especially during the first year after the dramatic changes in the family system, cause children's scholastic achievement to drop.

Threat to Self-Esteem

Whether continuous or temporary, or whether caused by failure in school, social life or in the family, low self-esteem often results from the pressures of divorce.

Many more factors exacerbate children's hardships. The proximity of divorce to additional losses and changes, such as a grandparent's death, emigration to a foreign country, birth of a baby in the family, sickness or disability, intensifies stress and diminishes internal coping resources. An environment of estrangement, which does not encourage and may even reject and stigmatise the child, jeopardises the already vulnerable youngster. The combination of physical disabilities, external and internal stress and lack of support is pernicious, because it subverts children's concept of their world as a safe place, as well as their perception of themselves as having control over their life and surroundings (Ayalon 1983).

The Influence of Age on Children's Reactions to Parental Divorce

Every child reacts differently to divorce, due to differences in personality, temperament, gender, life history and family structure. In addition, *age* is a factor whose influence must not be ignored. Difficulties are likely to arise when the divorce coincides with a new developmental stage in the child's life, such as weaning, starting school, or reaching adolescence.

In a follow-up study, Wallerstein and Kelly (1980) found that children's age at the time of divorce affected the quality and intensity of their responses. Each age and developmental stage had characteristic patterns. It is therefore hardly surprising that brothers and sisters, who undergo the experience of separation in the same family circumstances, differ in their reactions.

The divorce crisis's latent influences can appear many years later, when the child reaches a vulnerable stage of development (Hetherington 1981). Researchers have also found that the child's age at the time of study has greatly influenced the reaction to the divorce, even though the interview was held many years after the divorce (Francke 1983).

From Babyhood to Age Eight

The younger the child, the less concealed is his or her distress. Pre-school children suffer confusion and bewilderment, temporarily losing any independence they may already have achieved. They forget well-known words and concepts, and tend to see the disappearance of one parent as a signal that the other will disappear too. Children up to the age of eight are especially vulnerable and often regress to behaviour characteristic of much younger children, such as crying, wetting and having sleeping problems and imaginary fears. Young children express their feelings in the language of behaviour – in play and other non-verbal actions. Their patterns of playing in pre-school often become passive and rigid and they may stop using their creative imagination. They cling to adults and demand excessive approval and support, thus reducing their space for experimentation. Aggression against playmates causes social isolation, especially in boys, while girls tend to become introverted.

In most cases, the extreme reactions fade out approximately three years after the household breaks up, as each of the new and separate family systems stabilises. The stress signals most frequently observed during the post-divorce period include:

- Deep sorrow accompanied by images of death, destruction and desolation
- Feelings of deprivation, often manifested as an insatiable desire for food, presents, games and clothes
- Feelings of guilt, the child assuming blame for the divorce
- Wishful thinking and fantasies of family reunification, leading to denial of reality
- Indirect expression of anger towards the parents and its displacement onto friend and teachers.

From Age Nine Until Puberty

At a later age, the primary school child develops new ways of coping with losses. At this stage, children are more capable of expressing feelings of loneliness and shame to friends and teachers. Though some denial may appear, children experiment with active coping and search for sources of support outside the family.

Adolescence

In adolescence the crisis is likely to manifest itself in delinquency or depression. The characteristic expressions of the divorce crisis seen in teenagers are:

- Realistic fears, especially fears of further abandonment and poverty
- A better understanding of anger and its direct expression, accompanied by criticism of the parent considered 'guilty'
- Reduced feelings of responsibility and guilt for the divorce, replaced by fear for the welfare of the parents, as if parental and children's roles had been reversed
- Lack of concentration in school – in girls, this is often due to a tendency to day-dream about parental reconciliation, while boys, on the other hand, tend to take their anger and worry to extremes, to bicker with school authorities and to fight with their friends
- Conversely, the view that school is a refuge from their troubled home. Some adolescents invest all their energies in their studies to avoid thinking about what is happening in their families. Their school achievements are likely to camouflage their distress.
- A growing embarrassment concerning parents' sexual interests and their search for new partners. There is also jealousy of a parent's new friend or spouse.

- Distancing themselves from the storms at home and finding shelter in their social lives, which is a result of the relative independence of teenagers. An emotional attachment to a member of the opposite sex usually provides some compensation for family life.

At all ages, the conflict of divided loyalties creates major stress. Although children have a basic need for relationships with both parents, they may be expected to take sides in the dispute. As a result, they are torn between conflicting loyalties. Often, children exhibit the 'see-saw' phenomenon, characterised by radically different in-school and at-home behaviours. Some choose to release their fury and fears outside, while at home they behave obediently, so as not to endanger the relationship with the custodial parent. Others behave maturely at school, venting their anxieties at home, allowing themselves to cry and be angry.

Distress Signals

Not every child of divorce is in danger of being emotionally damaged. When the divorcing couple manage to separate their dispute from their parental role, and are able to agree on the best ways of fulfilling the child's needs, there is a better chance for the child to adapt to the new family systems and to develop appropriate relationship patterns.

Studies carried out three to five years after divorce (Raviv and Katzenelson 1986, Goetting 1981) maintain that children in intact families and children in divorced families often show no differences in learning ability, levels of achievement motivation, adaptation to school and development of delinquent behaviour. These findings lend themselves to two explanations. First of all, divorce is hardly the only cause of disturbance in children – children of intact families also show signs of distress and need help. Second, children generally need three to five years to recuperate from the divorce-generated upheaval and to regain their balance. This is a very long stretch – one third of childhood. During this period social relations, self-confidence and trust in others may be deeply affected.

A warning is warranted here. Even when it seems that a child is making a good adjustment, crisis may nevertheless appear during later developmental stages. Children who were very young during their parent's divorce and developed no symptoms at that juncture may develop learning and behaviour problems upon reaching adolescence (Johnston and Campbell 1988). Our clinical-educational experience confirms these findings. Even in cases where reactions to acute crises were not evident, signs of distress and suffering emerged at a later stage. These may result from various causes, ranging from expected developmental changes to additional traumatic losses.

All-Too-Common Scenarios

The following vignettes from school records show how distress signals express immediate and delayed difficulties facing children of divorce.

Alistair – Secondary Injury: Scapegoating

Alistair is eleven years old. His parents were divorced before he was born. One brother, ten years older than Alistair, is serving in the army and the other, the eldest, is married and lives in another city. When he was seven, his mother became ill and Alistair was sent to a residential home; however, his mother did not like living alone, and arranged for his return. He now lives with his mother and has never had any contact with his father. Recently, his teacher noticed that Alistair appeared very miserable and depressed, was very lonely in class and had stopped going out to the schoolyard with the other children. On investigation, she learned the following:

Earlier that year, Alistair and his mother had moved to a new house, where three of Alistair's classmates were living. He tried to make friends with them, but as they were all playing ball, a neighbour called out angrily: 'Don't play with Alistair, you shouldn't be friends with the likes of him'. When the man's children pressed him for an explanation, he said: 'His parents are divorced and he is no good'. Following this incident, the children snubbed Alistair in school and out, plunging him into profound loneliness.

The child, a victim of family circumstances, has had scapegoating added to his initial deprivation. His social environment has labled and ostracised him. Because of this 'secondary victimisation' (Symonds 1980), his chances for normal adaptation have been jeopardised.

When the secondary injury occurs in school, as in Alistair's case, it is the duty of school authorities to find appropriate solutions.

Michael – Injury to Self-Image

Michael is a slim, good-looking, twelve-year-old boy with black penetrating eyes. Other children at school want to be friends with him, but he prefers to be alone, and spends his breaks reading. The extensive reading has enriched Michael's vocabulary, but at the same time has erected an invisible wall between him and his peer group. In a serious heart-to-heart talk at one of the group-dynamics sessions, we learned of the sad world Michael had built in his imagination, a world in which he felt abandoned, disgusting and worthless, all because of his parents' divorce. He told the participants in the group:

> I know you want to help me, but someone whose parents are not divorced will never understand what I'm going through. Don't think I'm just an ordinary boy like all of you [*this was not a group specifically for children of divorce*]. With me everything's different. My mother and father don't live together. Even at my brother's Bar-Mitzvah party, which they

had at Grandma's (Dad's mother), my mother was not allowed to come. And now I'm worried all the time – what will happen at my Bar-Mitzvah...

Michael's negative self-image has led to extreme constriction of his social contacts. Yet his behaviour is also a call for help, which fortunately has been heard by the school counsellor.

Edward – the Child as Hostage

Edward is eight years old. His father has recently left home to live with another woman, who left her own son with her former husband. Edward's mother has suffered very much: her self-confidence and joy of living have been badly damaged. During the first stage of the separation, she became deeply depressed and needed therapy. She and her husband now fight at every opportunity, in Edward's presence and 'through' him. In the counsellor's presence, the father told Edward: 'You tell her how it really was – isn't it true that your mother is lying?'

The mother is permanently angry at Edward and beats him when he returns from visiting his father, for having played with 'that whore'. He is employed as a go-between, having to convey messages (which he often distorts) from one parent to the other. He is confused and has no idea what to expect. His mother urges him to carry her messages to the teacher; for example: 'Yesterday Father came home and broke a chair on Mother's legs. She told me to tell you'.

In class, Edward lies, disturbs the lessons and clings to the teacher.

The staff committee at school found that Edward has been using three behavioural patterns, acquired through active participation in family disputes, to manipulate his teachers in order to reduce his anxieties: first, instigating quarrels between the various people who take care of him at school (the class teacher and the school counsellor, for instance), second, drawing attention through dramatic acts, such as setting fires and third, holding on to people's personal belongings, to prevent them from leaving him. Edward has brought the family struggles into the school arena.

Sarah – Shackled by Learning Disability of Emotional Origin

Sarah, aged ten, is in the fourth year at junior school. During the first two years of school she was a bright and outstanding student; although she needed a lot of attention, she excelled in scholastic performance, perception and understanding. At the beginning of the third year, facial tics appeared, followed by eye-twitching. Attempts to discover the root of the problem were fruitless. Neither she nor her mother would talk. Her mother dismissed her child's difficulties as 'typical of a middle child', stuck between an older sister and a younger brother. At the end of the third year, Sarah's achievement at school began to deteriorate. Her handwriting become illegible, and copious spelling mistakes made it impossible to read her work. She stopped doing her homework and was not writing anything in class any more. Instead, she sharpened pencil after pencil and was perpetually looking for her exercise books and talking to her neighbours. She gradually turned into a serious problem in the class.

The school counsellor invited the mother to school, and they held some sessions together with Sarah. Only then did the truth emerge: the parents were on bad terms and had begun divorce proceedings. Sarah's father took to coming home late at night, leading to fights and mutual verbal abuse. Her mother forced Sarah to sit down and write out all the curses and slanders coming from her father's mouth, to be used as evidence in court. No wonder Sarah developed an emotional inhibition which affected her writing and spread to her other learning abilities. Dysgraphia, an inability to write, was, in Sarah's case, caused by emotional abuse. This symptom appeared to be a reaction to the unbearable role she had been assigned in her parents' conflict.

Mary – The Overburdened Child

Mary was six when her parents divorced. Her older brother was away from home at a boarding school and her father left, never to be heard from again. (Later it was discovered that he had been in a psychiatric hospital, suffering from a breakdown.) After the divorce, Mary's mother did less and less, leaving the child to fend for herself.

Noticing that Mary was exhausted at school, not concentrating and failing to master the intricacies of reading, the teacher asked to meet one of her parents. But, according to Mary: 'Father was abroad on business and Mother had to stay in bed, as she was pregnant and about to lose the baby...'

Having made a home visit, the social worker reported that Mary's mother was quite depressed. To make ends meet, she worked two shifts as a cook. Late each night she would return home, escorted by different men, and lock herself up in the bedroom. Mary had to carry the burden of shopping, laundering, preparing food and cleaning, with no one to listen to her and give her any support.

Mary is a typical example of 'the overburdened child syndrome', where parents, who may have been dysfunctional before the break-up, continue to be disorganised long after the divorce, unable to care properly for their children or meet the demands of family life (Wallerstein and Blakslee 1989).

Anna – The Parental Child: A Role Reversal

Anna, an eight-year-old girl, started daydreaming in school, declined in her scholastic performance and seemed very tense. After investigating the home scene, the counsellor found out that a few years earlier Anna's mother had started working outside the home to supplement the family's income. At work she met a married man who had three children of his own, and they struck up a friendship, staying at work later and later each day. Often the man brought her home in his car, and Anna, her younger brother and her father would watch them from the window sitting in the car and talking, sometimes for more then an hour. This 'friendship' led to the mother's demanding a divorce, complaining that she was unable to talk to the father, who bored her. The father moved out and the new friend moved in. The children remained with the mother, spending every second weekend with their father and paying him a short visit once a week. As they neared home on their journey back in the car, their father would burst out crying and Anna would have to comfort him. He then asked her to keep this scene a secret from her mother. At other times, he would start interrogating her about the 'friend' and about what was happening at home, flying into rage over the answers. Anna had to learn to stifle her own feelings, look after her father, keep things secret from him, and invent answers that were less 'dangerous'. She become increasingly listless at school and would not even play with the other children.

Anna had become a parental child and was psychologically overburdened. The responsibility she felt for her father, trying to protect and shield him from pain, was too heavy for her. It sapped her energy and she was not psychologically free to invest in her own development.

PART II

A HELPING HAND

CHAPTER FOUR

School
Home Away From Home

School as a Support System

When the family fails to provide its youngsters with a sound emotional and intellectual base because of its own psychological or socio-economical deficiencies, it is the school's responsibility to fulfil these needs. This unconventional demand, exacted by an international authority on rehabilitating the thought processes of deprived children, has challenged the old routines and dogmas of the educational system. Frankenstein (1966, 1970, 1981) has devised teacher-oriented intervention methods to improve the intellectual condition of deprived children and adolescents, a great number of whom come from divorced and dysfunctional families. It has been conclusively proven that post-divorce changes have six major aversive effects which are noticeable in school (Thompson *et al.* 1984):

1. Reluctance to disclose divorce-related stress and abuse.

2. Decline in academic performance in reading, mathematics and language skills.

3. Changes in concentration level (e.g. daydreaming).

4. Changes in ability to communicate with teachers or peers.

5. Sudden alienation or withdrawal from others.

6. Increased aggressiveness.

In many cases, school authorities cannot rely on the parents to cooperate by imposing discipline or monitoring the performance of homework. Roles are frequently reversed, and the school becomes responsible for defending the child from violence and neglect at home. There are cases where the school is asked to mediate between the child and the parents. Increasingly, the school is expected to take over the parenting role, sometimes even to see that children are fed, nurturing them and lending a ready ear, so that their emotional needs are met. At other times, the school becomes a battlefield for the antagonistic parents. Each one tries to persuade the teacher or headteacher that his or her version of what goes on at home is the true one, in order to gain a sympathetic ally. Mothers and fathers who have nobody to confide in turn to the teacher to assist them in their parental roles and share their concern for the child. Some involve the school in the struggle between them, with one parent demanding that no information regarding the child's behaviour, problems or achievements at school be disclosed to the other parent. Often the reason for this is that the custodial parent does not wish to be exposed to the other parent's criticism. When a court order restricts the meetings of one parent with the children, the schoolyard may turn into a 'secret meeting place', and there have even been incidents of children 'kidnapped' from school by an embittered parent.

The child's distress becomes evident at school through many and varied symptoms: learning problems, difficulty in concentrating, daydreaming and exhaustion (Felner, Farber and Primavera 1980, Wallerstein 1983). Such symptoms are very similar to those of 'combat stress reaction' (Noy 1991). They result in failure in exams, inconsistency in homework, tardiness in coming to school and absenteeism. Anxious children who suffer from insomnia fall asleep in the middle of lessons.

An angry and anxious child, whose tolerance threshold is very low, easily becomes a target of other children's teasing. The stigma that clings to a child of divorce 'invites' social rejection which may escalate into actual abuse. Instead of achieving relief from tension and getting moral support away from the family battle-ground, children find themselves fighting on yet another front.

> If I've gone down in my studies
> It isn't my fault.
> I simply just can't.
> I'm scared – all the time –
> That the children in class will ask me:
> > 'Where's your dad?',
> And
> > 'Is your mother divorced?'
>
> (S. Raviv)

Sometimes the teacher is the only adult that children can turn to, when adults within the family have failed them. A teacher may become the only consistent identification model in these difficult times. Isolated and lonely children may develop dependency relationships as a way of getting special attention. If teachers support such children, they may rescue them from being swallowed up by the family crisis, and enable them to succeed in their various tasks at school.

Allers (1982) points out that the life of children of divorced parents is uncertain and unpredictable. The only place that remains consistent and reliable for them, enabling them to feel safe, is school. Here, the day-to-day life is predictable, the bell rings regularly and the time-table is fixed. The teacher too is predictable in his or her recurring demands of the pupils. For this reason, a change of teachers can often be detrimental for those children who are in need of constancy in their lives.

It is imperative that schools develop new ways of educational intervention that will help such children to improve their situation. It is vital not to hurt them any more. At the administrative level, the school system has to reach decisions that take into account the changing structure of pupils' families: should two 'Letters to Parents' be sent simultaneously to two different addresses? Should each parent be invited separately to discuss the child's progress at school? Which of the two should be invited to parties and celebrations, as well as the end of the school year? Which of the two should be invited to accompany a class trip? These questions become difficult to answer when there is no agreement or co-operation between the parents over issues involving the school.

Recommendations for School Policy Concerning Contact with Divorced Parents

In the event of any problem arising between separated parents and the educational system, it is suggested that the following procedures be followed:

1. If the classroom teacher learns (from any reliable source) that a child's parents have separated, instituted divorce proceedings, or divorced, she or he should inform the headteacher and the school counsellor immediately.

2. If a parent approaches the school about the separation or the divorce, the class teacher should invite the psychologist to meet with both parents, or with each parent separately. This is mainly to obtain information about facts pertaining to the children and their relationships with their parents.

3. If a judicial settlement has determined the custody of the child, the headteacher or class teacher should ask for copy of this ruling. After having received it, the school should act according to the decision regarding relationships with the parents. If the ruling stipulates that the rela-

tionship between the non-custodial parent and the child should continue, the parent should apply in writing to the school in order to receive reports on the child's progress in studies and behaviour.

4. If school personnel have any questions about the meaning, implications or validity of the ruling, the headteacher should be advised by legal counsel.

5. The school's daily contacts should be with the custodial parent. Additionally, having received permission from the custodial parent, the school should enable the non-custodial parent to have a say in educational decisions concerning the child, within the limitations mandated by the court's ruling.

6. Where questions arise about either parent's rights and roles in the parent-school relationship, educators should consult with the school therapist (guidance counsellor, psychologist, etc.) or with community mental health workers associated with the school.

Many schools show flexibility by being prepared to write down both fathers' and mothers' telephone numbers and addresses at home and at work, for use in cases of emergency.

Attitudes Toward Divorced Families, as Reflected in School Policies and Curricula

Do the educational authorities carry out the new duties expected of them? In a chapter titled 'School – The Second Family of the Child of Divorce', Francke (1983) mentions a survey of headteachers' and inspectors' attitudes that shows both extremely positive and extremely negative attitudes towards this subject. Those who are against school involvement in mental health issues point out the lack of financial resources, lack of professional mental health personnel, and teachers' lack of knowledge about and orientation to the problems of divorce. To back up their reluctance, teachers cite excessive workloads, standard conservative definitions of the teacher's role and fear of getting involved with the law (such as when teachers are asked to appear in court as witnesses in custody cases). Other reservations are due to the fact that divorce is one of those subjects veiled in a conspiracy of silence that does not allow open communication, similar to the taboos surrounding bereavement, disability and sex (Ayalon 1979a). Teachers avoid mentioning the subject because they are afraid of hurting or shaming children. Others fear the anger of parents who might consider the teacher's concern with divorce interference in their personal business. The failure of many teachers to address the pupil's special situation can be explained by their anxiety over the fact that crisis in the family is spreading throughout society. Divorced teachers who are themselves parents may have a vested interest in proving that children are not at all vulnerable to or hurt by their parents' divorce.

Few existing curricula encourage treatment of the subject of divorce. Many of the readers, which are the main source of the child's encounter with ideas, values and subjects, systematically refrain from dealing with subjects connected with existential stress. They also avoid problems of crisis in the family, missing the opportunity to offer children validation of their 'nonstandard' and some-times bizarre experiences. Curricula that discriminate against the basic needs of the children fail to use classroom learning as a springboard for development of coping skills for times of stress (Bettleheim and Zelan 1982). An Israeli study (Flasher 1984) of the degree to which readers used in the primary grades reflect existential problems faced by children found that divorce did not appear in any. In all the surveyed readers, the family was portrayed only in the traditional pattern of father, mother and biological children. Patterns of alternative families (adoptive families, one–parent families, families blended through remarriage, step-parents and stepbrothers) were not represented whatsoever. For children who grow up in such families, this is a distorted reflection of social reality – and the number of these families is increasing very rapidly. Children experiencing the various stages of separation and divorce are thus deprived of the chance to examine their problems in the legitimate setting of their studies and their peer group.

It is not surprising, therefore, that children of divorce are ashamed of their situation and feel that they have to hide it, lie about it and deny it so as to adapt themselves to normative expectations. The class as a social group misses the opportunity to develop tolerance for a variety of lifestyles and to provide support and mutual help.

Lately, however, there has been a breakthrough in this matter. Schools are preparing themselves to work with stress and engage in intervention in times of crisis at system, group and individual levels (Ayalon 1979b). Special mental health programmes are being introduced into school syllabi. *Rescue! Helping Children Cope with Stress* (Ayalon 1992), *Looking Ahead at Life's Options: Suicide Prevention* (Ayalon and Lahad 1992), *Values Clarification* (Shechtman 1980) and *Magic Circle* (in Palamores and Ball 1980) are several examples of such stress inoculation programmes. School-initiated crisis intervention following terrorist attacks on school children have brought immediate relief and prevented post-traumatic disorders (Ayalon 1987, 1993). Plans for helping children of divorce developed along the same lines: a few schools have introduced programs dealing with families, marriage and divorce, as well as bereavement and separation. In some schools the pupils themselves initiated peer support groups. In one of these schools, the students created a film about the problems facing children of divorce out of their own experiences.

During these school-sponsored activities, children learn from one another how to survive their parents' divorce. They exchange information that nobody has bothered to give them about their rights. They find out to whom to turn – psychologists, lawyers, judges – from their friends' recommendations.

These activities are sometimes met with opposition from all sides: peers who are fed up with the subject and seek diversions when they are away from their troubled homes; parents who are afraid their secrets will become public knowledge; parents who do not trust the professional qualifications of teachers; teachers who are afraid of 'labelling' the children; headteachers who are worried about the heavy burden on the school budget and also fear possible parental resistance.

However, given the fact that school is sometimes the only constant factor in the lives of so many children, it is impossible, in the long run, to avoid accepting responsibility for attending to the needs of pupils from divorced families. In addition to making administrative changes, revising school text books and increasing the number of hours given to helping activities, the authorities will have to widen the spectrum of school services over and above the hours allotted to teaching. They will have to take responsibility and intervene in pupils' families, when necessary; among other things, school may have to care for and feed the children of working mothers. If these areas are neglected, academic activities will also be jeopardised.

There is an easily available reservoir of helping services for mental health in the educational system. Among them are teachers, therapeutic and resource teachers and counsellors. In addition, school staff are assisted by professionals such as social workers, truancy officers, nurses, psychologists and doctors. All these can give valuable help to children of divorce.

Target Populations for Intervention

We can identify four different target populations for intervention within schools:

- Individual children who show symptoms of distress because of a crisis in the family
- The child's peer-group – in order to prevent 'anxiety of contagion' and social ostracism of children of divorce
- Teachers who come in contact with children of divorce, and need training
- Parents of children who are participating in the programme, and themselves need guidance.

Levels of Intervention

All intervention is preventive, for it intrinsically aims to reduce pathology. Many preventive programmes, whether geared to community stresses in time of crisis or to family and individual stresses due to divorce-related crises, are based upon the patterns set in Caplan's classical model (Caplan 1964). According to this model, there are three distinctive and critical types of intervention, each appropriate to a particular phase of the crisis.

1. *Preventive intervention.* The main function of this is to estimate, differentiate and appraise the threat cues, using both solid information and the foresight born of experience.

2. *Crisis intervention.* This is immediate and, as far as possible, practical, whether the crisis is short-term or prolonged. The aims of the intervention are to enhance judgement and discrimination, to point out directions for activities that enable immediate relief and to strengthen adaptive behaviour.

3. *Therapeutic-rehabilitative intervention.* This takes place in the aftermath of the crisis and aims to reduce post-traumatic effects.

The programme outlined in the Comprehensive Model (Chapter 5) and described in detail (Chapters 6–13) is designed for the multiple purposes of inoculation, prevention of future disturbances, and treatment of immediate difficulties. It is based on assessment of the various crisis stages in the divorce process. Each step of the programme provides a generalised description of the stresses, threats and demands triggered by the numerous losses and changes in daily lives, social contacts, and parental relationships. The stages do not necessarily correspond to given points in time, but call attention to the appropriate therapeutic goals and the suggested modes of treatment.

The crisis of divorce is naturally a prolonged process, with the end of one stage often leading into the beginning of a new one. The target population is therefore heterogeneous in terms of the timing of the crisis in the life of the child. Children participating in the same group will be going through various stages of the crisis, making it difficult to distinguish clearly at which of the three levels to intervene. Group facilitators are invited to use their own judgement in choosing the activities suitable for the individual and/or the group.

The recommended skills for facilitators are:

- Thorough familiarity with and understanding of diagnostic and therapeutic-rehabilitative mental health approaches
- Qualification as a facilitator of group-dynamics
- Understanding of stress, stress-inoculation and coping skills.

The programme's approach is holistic. It tries to tap the resources of the cognitive, imaginative, affective, physical and social facets of the personality.

Methods of intervention reflect the Multi-Modal orientation practiced within a group-setting, individual or family meetings. Creative writing, role-playing, bibliotherapy, values-clarification, transactional analysis and self-control development trigger the imagination and enable participants to identify with different role-models. These methods arouse involvement and help children express concealed feelings. They develop empathy and understanding of other people's situations, along with self-acceptance.

CHAPTER FIVE

A Comprehensive Model for Interventions Designed to Help Children Cope With Divorce-Related Crises and Problems

Stages of Coping and Methods of Intervention

The table which follows is divided into two columns. The left-hand column (*Chain Reactions Set Off By Parental Divorce*) is divided into four subcolumns, which respectively name each stage, detail the stresses likely to arise, describe children's possible reactions, and delineate the therapeutic aims which arise from the diagnoses set out in the previous subcolumn. The right-hand column (*Methods of Intervention*) presents stage-appropriate activities for the therapeutic group.

It is important to emphasise that both the classification of children's reactions and the means of intervention are suggested here as a blueprint only. Each case has different dynamics and requires a different approach. The interventions are based on a structured open- ended model: the stimulus is introduced by the leader and the products flow directly from the participants' reactions. This approach facilitates the group process without inhibiting personal expression.

Chain Reactions Set Off by Parental Divorce

Stage	Stress or Demand	The Child's Reaction	Therapeutic Goals
Stage I *Ambiguity and imbalance*	Threat to family stability	Reawakening of separation anxiety	Enhancing children's ability to endure ambiguous situations
	Uncertainty regarding family continuity	Oscillation of moods	Rescuing children from no-win situations, by fortifying external support systems
	Passive and active participation in parents' conflict	Confusion and daydreaming	Providing pleasant activities, to divert children's minds from their troubles
	Enforced keeping of family secrets	blocked learning capacity, due to efforts invested in 'not knowing' or in keeping secrets	
Stage II *Denial*	Loss of status; social isolation	Tendency to avoid responsibilities and social interaction	Reinforcing social support
	Threatened loss of a parent and changes in child's place in the family (experienced as loss)	Confusion, grief and fantasies about family reunification	Children's awareness and acceptance of unavoidable changes
			Facilitation of children's self-expression
	Handicapped self-concept; feeling 'different' and/or stigmatised		Rehabilitation of self-concept and of belief that child can hold on to his or her place in society

Methods of Intervention

Creating the group	Selection of members; getting acquainted; setting rules; learning communications skills; developing vocabulary for effective communication of feelings; creating a pleasant atmosphere
Exercise in visual perception	Use of stimulus in which 'figure' and 'ground' are interchangeable, in order to strengthen tolerance for ambiguity
Values clarification (VC)	Sentence completions describing confusion and embarrassment

Free writing	Aimed at encouraging expression of feelings and enabling discussions with the help of pictures depicting, for example, families, a child with only one parent, a lonely child, a child who is 'different'
Values clarification (VC)	Sentence completions and questions for discussion about possible connections between a child's feelings and the situation at home: daydreaming; nightmares; loss of appetite, etc.
Role-playing	The group role-plays family scenes described by a member
Bibliotherapy	Presentation and discussion of a story that features denial reactions toward parental separation

Chain Reactions Set Off by Parental Divorce

Stage	Stress or Demand	The Child's Reaction	Therapeutic Goals
Stage III Self-blame	Feeling guilty about parental separation	Expressions of guilt; nightmares; physical symptoms	To teach 'reality testing', which reduces guilt
	Self-attribution of destructive forces	Seeking punishment and inflicting self-punishment	To reduce 'magical thinking' (feelings of omnipotence)
	Feeling torn between parents' demands for loyalty	Not eating; 'inviting' failure in studies and social life	
Stage IV Anger	Frustration due to real losses and violation of promises	Verbal hostility against adults; aggression towards children and objects	Channelling anger, by providing physical and verbal outlets for it
	Being 'scapegoated' Passing from self-blame to blame of parents and society	Disturbances in classroom; outbursts of fury	Learning the 'Self-Control' method
	Jealousy of other children	Pent-up anger, expressed as submissiveness	
	Jealousy of parent's new mate, as defense against despair	Fear of anger and the punishment it incurs, leading to clinging to and overdependency on parent	Understanding oneself and accepting feelings; Understanding parents' motivations and situations

Methods of Intervention

Bibliotherapy	Dealing with negative self-image through poems and stories written about children of divorced parents
Transactional analysis (TA)	Helping children distinguish between blame ('Parent' ego-state) and vengefulness ('Child' ego-state), as opposed to responsibility for oneself and one's actions ('Adult' ego-state)
Values clarification (VC)	Use of pictures and sentence completions (among other exercises) for clarifying parents' responsibility for their divorce. (For example, one picture shows two adults quarreling and a child asking himself: 'What did I do to them?')

Using colour and other primarily nonverbal media	Expressing anger in personal and group painting. Dramatic creation of situations, using body language to encourag expressions of anger. Channelling of anger by using rules in anger games. Creating group norms that confirm feelings of anger
Games	Reflecting existing and desired proximity among family members by placing figures, toy animals, stones, or other small objects on a board
Self-control	1. Teaching/encouraging discrimination between thought and action 2. Giving reinforcement for positive thinking 3. Demonstrating changing behaviour by changing thoughts
Transactional analysis (TA)	Using the principles of TA to understand parents' temporary dysfunction while under stress. Learning how to 'put oneself in one's parents' shoes' to understand their viewpoints

Chain Reactions Set Off by Parental Divorce

Stage	Stress or Demand	The Child's Reaction	Therapeutic Goals
Stage V *Despair*	Fear of losing the remaining parent	Psychosomatic illnesses; psychogenic	Support and encouragement
	Cumulative effect of familial, social and economic losses; loss of pleasures;	accidents and wounds	Social compensations, as substitute for losses in the family
	loss of attention	Regressive reactions; crying; failure in studies and social	Finding satisfying new activities
	Loss of hope for parental reunification	activities	Building a positive self- concept
Stage VI *Coping*	Acceptance of new identity and reality of divorce	Open-mindedness towards new experiences	Rehearsal of situations that the child may experience, e.g., additional losses, parental remarriage(s), etc.
	Coming to terms with the new situation	Active search for solutions	Looking for new 'meaning in life'
	Threats to the child's status in the new family systems, due to parental remarriage(s) or moving to a new home	Demands for overcompensation	Learning ways of communication to facilitate contact with new family members

Methods of Intervention

- Enhancing group cohesiveness

- Relaxation exercises and positive suggestion

- Creative work, using diverse art forms

- Use of the 'feelings wheel' to improve awareness of
- changes in mood

- Expansion of 'ego boundaries', through exercises of the
- imagination ('If only...)

- Enhancing hope for the future, through imagination,
- planning, etc.

Values clarification (VC)	Suggestions for positive activities and exploration of social obligations, to enhance coping
Self-control	Thought – Feeling – Action: Using card-games suggesting active coping attitudes and behaviours
'Creative thinking'	Inventing alternative solutions to possible and impossible situations
Role-playing	Dramatisation of situations connected to parental remarriage

PART III

MIND OVER MATTER

CHAPTER SIX

The Healing Metaphor

The Psychological Dynamics of Metaphor

Written words have influenced the attitudes, decisions and behaviour of humankind since the beginning of recorded history. As people became aware that the written word could influence behaviour, they began to develop ways to apply this power. The use of reading material to help solve emotional problems and promote mental health became known as bibliotherapy, and claimed its place among the arts therapies. The term 'bibliotherapy' comes from Greek: 'biblion' means 'book' and 'therapy' means 'service' (Moustakas 1959). As a preventive therapy for cognitive, emotional and behaviour disorders, bibliotherapy is an ancient art in modern dress. An inscription over a library in ancient Thebes proclaimed it 'the Healing Place of the Soul.' Turning to literature, poetry and drama as a source for ideas, solace and guidance has always been a productive practice. The Bible is replete with stories and parables that have shaped people's lives and still do, and Greek drama has been a massive emotional catalyst.

Shiryon, a pioneer bibliotherapist, quotes Robert Graves' recommendation (1978): 'A well chosen anthology is a complete dispensary of medicine for the more common mental disorders and may be used for prevention as for cure.' Guided by the therapist, the interaction between person and text may contribute to self-knowledge and self-esteem, assuage unconscious conflicts, clarify values and increase empathy.

Bibliotherapy has been adapted for practice in schools as a mental hygiene preventive measure for the general child-population (Kubovi 1992), and as a curative device for high-risk populations, such as children who suffer bereavement, divorce, abuse or disabilities (Ayalon and Lahad 1990, 1992, Lahad 1984, 1992).

The healing power of bibliotherapy lies in its power to arouse deep-seated processes such as identification, projection and insight.

Identification

The child may identify with a character or a situation within the text because of their affinity to the child's inner experience or outer circumstances. The realisation that others share similar predicaments is followed by an immediate feeling of relief: 'Here I am, and I am not alone.' Children often identify with characters in animal stories as well as with fictional beings, when the animals have believable human traits. Fictional characters can become ideal role models for youngsters who are deprived of positive relations with adults.

Projection

Children tend to project their hopes and frustrations onto fictional characters, and then reclaim these very same feelings. The story therefore becomes a mirror, safely reflecting both virtues and drawbacks of the reader, without presenting a direct threat of social sanction. When actual feelings such as love, hate, anger, fear or jealousy, which are directed toward a significant person, are projected onto the character in the story, they can be dealt with from a safe distance. This distance allows children to mobilise psychological energies in order to broaden their repertoires of coping behaviours.

Shy and apprehensive children, who dare not voice their complaints directly, may discuss their projected feelings openly, in the safety created by this fiction. A sensitive therapist will allow the discussion to remain within the metaphor and will not try to bring the child back to the harsh truths of reality (Flasher 1984).

Insight

Insight is considered the pinnacle of the therapeutic experience. Individuals gain fresh understanding and self-awareness of their motives, needs and entanglements while working through vicarious conflicts and watching themselves in the mirror provided by the many facets of a well chosen story. The overt, rational meaning is absorbed consciously, whilst the hidden meaning, enfolded in metaphors, analogies, and similes, is absorbed intuitively. The tale can be acknowledged, heard and received, and then left behind, trusting that the unconscious itself will gradually help to integrate the material into the client's awareness of Self (Gersie 1991).

Choosing the Healing Metaphor

The resources for bibliotherapy are abundant. We draw from written literature and oral traditions of tales, myth and mythology. We use different literary forms such as prose, poetry and drama, fiction and non-fiction. The stories are presented in a structured framework from which the therapeutic motifs embedded in the stories emerge. Finding the right story for a specific therapeutic intervention is of great importance. Bettelheim (1976) gives us some general guidelines:

> For a story truly to hold the child's attention, it must entertain him and arouse his curiosity. But to enrich his life, it must stimulate his imagination; help him to develop his intellect and to clarify his emotions; be attuned to his anxieties and aspirations; give full recognition to his difficulties, while at the same time suggesting solutions to the problems that perturb him. In short, it must at one and the same time relate to all aspects of his personality... giving full credence to the seriousness of the child's predicaments, while simultaneously prompting confidence in himself and in his future. (p.5)

These therapeutic qualities are often found in folk-tales and fairy-tales that excite the imagination, exaggerate the conflicts between 'good' and 'evil' and do not evade existential problems (Shenhar-Elroi 1986). The barriers of blatant taboos or discreet prohibitions against touching forbidden subject are thus removed.

Storytelling in Therapy

Storytelling is a powerful tool for working through crises. A story told or read can become a key experience in dealing with inner stress and external hardships. 'Stories pass from one generation to the next, bearing witness to the ordering of knowledge, providing the distilled wisdom of each age for those to come' (Gersie and King 1990). Story-work is suitable for children at every age and also for the 'child' within each of us, who surrenders and reacts to the magic of words, symbols, rhyme and rhythm. Active modes of storytelling invite children to become active participants, by dramatisation, adding bits to the story, singing, painting, role-playing and writing.

Following are some guidelines for setting up a storytelling session.

1. The storyteller should create a relaxed and secure environment.

2. A rhythmic pattern or chant may be repeated by the storyteller.

3. The storyteller should use the art of improvisation, presenting the story in a dramatic and vivid manner.

4. The storyteller should be sensitive to the listeners' non-verbal cues, weaving the story responsively and involving the audience through touch and eye contact.

5. The storyteller should allow enough space for participants to move, act, tell or write their own story.

Applying the Healing Structure

Telling, retelling and weaving personal motifs into indigenous tales changes and transforms them. The following story is an example of such a transformation, retold from memory by one of us (Adina Flasher). The transformed story then travelled through groups of children, who came for therapy to recuperate from the traumatic collapse of their home and hearth. Two focal themes emerged in these groups: 'breach of confidence' and 'home-sickness.' The structure has been adapted from Gersie and King (1990). The original story appears in Gersie (1991, p.254.)

The Star Girl

Far, far away, beyond the blue skies, lived the Star people. They were always busy helping each other and helping anyone they could. They were very happy. Once in a blue moon they unrolled their milky, star-studded carpet, and, twinkling happily, they would climb up and down this shiny carpet-ladder and help the people on Earth. This went on for a whole month.

Little Star-Girl was very excited – this was the first time that she too was to go on a journey. She put on her beautiful star-dress, prepared herself for the journey and kissed her mother good-bye. Her mother handed her a basket, and said, 'Whatever happens, never, ever, let anyone look inside the basket. Never let anyone open it.' The star-girl promised, excitedly skipping down the star-ladder.

At this point, the children are asked to draw the basket just as they imagine it, and, when they are finished, to place it in front of them for all the group-members to see.

In the meantime, far, far away on Earth, lived some people. They were good and hardworking people who worked the earth, tilled the soil, saw to their cows and sheep and worked hard for their living. That year they had been working very, very, hard for their existence as there had been a drought in the land. One morning a lonely man who lived all alone in his hut got up and noticed that all his cows had been milked.

'What's this?' he cried. 'Who did this? Oh, and look, all the hay has been tossed, and the sheep have been fed, and the eggs collected.'

But nobody answered.

The following morning, and the morning after that, the same surprise awaited him: the cows had been milked and fed, the hay tossed, and the eggs collected!

Deciding to find out what all this was about, the man did not go to sleep that night. He hid himself in the barn, and waited to see what would happen. Lo and behold, as soon as the moon appeared he saw gorgeous creatures twinkling around his barn, busily working and getting all his chores done. He was astounded. He watched them, gaping all the time. His eyes rested on a specially beautiful one. It was Star-Girl. Just as they were about to leave, the man caught Star-Girl and begged her not to go with the others, but to stay with him. 'I live here all alone, I'm so lonely and have nobody to speak to. Please, please stay with me,' he begged.

'All right,' said Star-Girl, 'but on one condition: that you never, ever, look into my basket. Promise me that you'll never peep into my basket – that you'll never open it.' The man promised readily and from that day they lived together in his little hut.

They did all the work together, and kept the little hut tidy. They were quite content, but sometimes, at night, when the stars were shining, Star-Girl started thinking of home and wondering what her people were doing. She longed for them, but she also knew that the man needed her very much. One night, when the man was asleep, she again started thinking of the Star Kingdom and decided to write someone a letter.

The children now become Star-Girl. They can write the letter to anyone they wish – a relative, a friend, or any real or imaginary figure.

After the children have written the letter, they are asked to fold the page carefully and to put it in a basket that is passed around. They are told: 'In a magical way this letter reaches its destination. Please pick a letter from the basket. If it happens to be your own, please return it. Read the letter and answer it in the name of the person to whom it has been written. Please consider the feelings and thoughts that have been expressed in the letter and answer them'.

After finishing their answers, the children are instructed to fold them inside the original letter, leaving the original handwriting outside. This makes it easier for each person to identify and reclaim his or her original letter together with the response.

The stories are then read aloud and shared with the whole group, before returning to the original tale.

One day, Star-Girl went out with the sheep. She walked for many miles, and was late coming back. When she returned, she noticed that her basket was in a peculiar position. Her heart pounding, she turned to the man and said:

'You've opened the basket... you've looked inside...'

'So what?...'

'But you promised, you really and truly promised...'

'Don't be stupid, there was nothing inside it...'

The children then write an ending to the story, which again they can share with the group. The fact that the children become involved in shaping the story and actively participate in it 'invites the interweaving of individual and collective experiences, and the creation of new products' (Gersie 1984). The themes related to divorce in this story are very powerful for working with children who are undergoing the upheaval and soul-searching of wondering whom they can trust, separation, longing, loneliness and double loyalty. The activities and the process involved in the storytelling enable the children to work through their conflicts within the metaphor.

Bibliotherapy and Biblio-Guidance

Children's literature offers a wide variety of material for bibliotherapy for children of divorce, ranging from authentic poems and tales that have intrinsic value and psychological validity to prescriptive, tailor-made stories with limited therapeutic potential. 'Divorce literature' for children also includes straightforward non-fiction guidebooks. In their quest for knowledge and need for some kind of impartial authority, children in distress absorb whatever is available. Often, unpretentious publications have proven to be of value to both parents and teachers, as triggers for touching upon issues regarding divorce.

Separation From a Parent

Animal stories speak directly to the uninitiated child. Some modern animal stories are written for the purpose of biblio-guidance with very small children of divorce. The following story is a typical example of this kind. 'Zebra-Zebroni' (Burla 1968) is a very popular story, depicting a seemingly simplified version of parental separation and remarriage. The story makes use of familiar fairy-tale elements: It begins with an unexplained disappearance of the mother and concludes with a sort of 'happy end.' Within this framework, a modern story of a child's coping with the stress of divorce is presented. The young Zebroni witnesses violent signs of his parents' emotional divorce and separation. Left to himself without solace or support, he runs away from home. He is not missed or cared for by his preoccupied and angry father. His predicament is compounded by the his friends' desertion. Neglected, angry and depressed, he might have fallen apart completely were it not for a guide, the turtle, who teaches him to be self-sufficient. In the process of maturation, young Zebroni moves from needing help to offering it, and accepts (a bit too readily) his father's new mate.

The story is told to a group of early learners, who bring their own experiences to the fore.

Zebra Zebroni, by Oded Burla

Once upon a time there was a zebra. The zebra was exactly like all the other zebras, with a tail and ears and black and white stripes – but this zebra was still very tiny. His name was Zebroni. Every day he used to go for long walks with Daddy-Zebra and Mummy-Zebra, having so much fun that he would jump around, being mischievous and unruly. He was always happy. Only one thing made him sad: sometimes Daddy-Zebra and Mummy-Zebra had a quarrel. Sometimes they even kicked each other a little, or bit each other...

Whenever Zebroni's parents started quarreling, he was very sad and ran away, finding somewhere to hide. He didn't like to see them fight with each other.

One day, when he came out of the place where he had hidden after a very big fight, he saw only his father.

'Where's my mummy?' he asked.

'She isn't here – she's gone,' answered his father angrily.

'When will she be back?' asked Zebroni.

'It doesn't matter!' said Daddy-Zebra...

'So who will feed me?' worried Zebroni.

'I will,' said Daddy-Zebra.

'But you don't know how to feed me!'

'Oh I do, I do. I know everything!' said Daddy-Zebra.

'So why don't you lick me, like Mummy does?'

'Because – because I'm busy now. I'm thinking. Don't bother me.'

'My mummy never told me that I bother her!' said Zebroni in a rage.

He decided to be unruly and a bit mischievous, but he was sad, so he jumped only once and was mischievous only once – and stopped. 'Oh...,' he said to himself, 'How I miss Mother now that she has gone away!' He cried a lot and was very sad. Daddy-Zebra looked after Zebroni, but he didn't know how to do all the things that Mummy-Zebra used to do. Then the other little zebras, Zebroni's friends, started leaving him. They said that he wasn't clean and that he wasn't tidy. They added that he wasn't fun to be with any more. And they teased him and told him that his mother had run away. And it was all true. Zebroni envied all his friends for having whole families, and then he even began to get angry at his mother – to grow further and further away from her. He was always alone, and always sad.

The days passed, and Zebroni grew and grew. And one day, when he wasn't so very tiny any more, he met a turtle standing on top of a hill singing the song of the turtles. He sang in a clear but trembling voice:

> The turtle's sad
> And also mad
> 'Cause of times he's had
> But he isn't bad
> The turtle...

The turtle stopped singing. He saw Zebroni.

'Why are you sad?' he asked. You see, this was a clever turtle.

'I have some problems...' answered Zebroni.

'Tell me your problems,' said the turtle. 'Maybe I can help you. What happened?'

Zebroni thought for a moment and then asked:

'Where's your mother?'

'What???' cried the turtle, his voice becoming somewhat hoarse. 'I don't have one! I've never had one! And I'll never have one!'

'But how can that be?' asked Zebroni unbelievingly. 'Who looked after you when you were little? Who licked you?'

The turtle covered his ears and shut his eyes and then said:

'First of all, I'm not so big yet... and secondly, I don't like to be looked after or licked! What am I, a baby? What, can't I find grass that I love to eat by myself? What, can't I find water to drink for myself? What, can't I clean myself a little? What...'

'Hold it, hold it!' said Zebroni. 'What did you say before – that you've never had a mother???'

'That's right. I haven't.'

'So – how... who... from where...?

'All right,' said the turtle with a kind smile. 'I'll explain it to you. With us it's different. Mummy-Turtle lays eggs somewhere and goes off on her way, to another country, to another field – anywhere she likes. After a while the eggs are hatched and tiny little turtles come out. They say hello – because they are very polite. Then they say: 'I'll be seeing you,' and each and every one goes his own way to begin a new life. Each one finds his own food, his own water and his fun – and that's that, he becomes a turtle, just like me, for instance. We learn to get along without mothers. All alone. We are already big – even when we are small!!'

'I think you've solved my problem.' said Zebroni. 'Thank you, Turtle.' Zebroni went away and thought: 'It's true that it's much better to have a whole family – a father as well as a mother as well as Zebroni, but if there isn't a whole family to be had, you have to make do with what you do have. I have a father and I abandoned him. That isn't very nice.'

Zebroni looked for his father: When he found him, he saw that he was walking with a lady zebra, who was not his mother.

'Ah,' said Zebroni to his father, 'I see that you are not alone anymore, and you have someone to look after you. I've learned to look after myself – and I've come to help you.'

'Ho, ho!' said his father: 'Since when does a son look after his father?' 'Ho, ho!' said Zebroni. 'Ever since the son has learned to look after himself.'

From then on they all become friends – Zebroni, his father, Mrs. Zebra, who was like a new mother, and later the little new Zebronino who was born – his brother. And all the friends who had left Zebroni came back and became friends again, and they lived happily ever after. Well, almost...

Pain and Humour

The pain experienced during the family break-up may be too hard for a child to endure. Various means of denial are employed by children who try to hold their head above water. Humour, quite often black humour, is a helpful mechanism, masking anger and guilt. Much like dreaming, the process of creating humour very often uses different manoeuvres such as surprise, paradox, misperception and bending reality, reversal and intentional invention of mischief. The aggressive function of humour feeds our feeling of superiority over others, making them look ridiculous and thus less threatening.

Tilly Tall-Tale (Ben-Ezer 1979) is one of those mischievous girls or boys who take it all out on grownups. No wonder adults don't like the story very much, while children adore it! But it is not all fun. Through the screen of pranks, Tilly's emotional pain is rather obvious.

Tilly Tall-Tale, by Ehud Ben-Ezer

When Dad divorced Mum I was the happiest girl in the world. I slept with Mum in the big bed, on Dad's side. And Mum bought me a new dress and new black shining shoes, and Dad bought me a new watch. Everyday I was as excited as if it were my birthday.

All the children were jealous of me for having an onlyness mother. (I know you should say 'a separate' mother and 'a separate' father, but once Mum heard me say 'an onlyness Mummy' and she thought it was cute, and she said: 'That's right, Tilly, I am alone now that your Dad has left and I have only you. We both are lonely. We are now each other's only true family!')

The psychologist told me that I now have to treat both Mum and Dad very nicely because it's very hard for them to be 'onlynesses.'

So now, to make them forget their sadness for being 'onlynesses,' I ask them many riddles, and tell them all sorts of jokes that are funny, especially for people who are lonely. For instance:

What is green, whistles and sometimes limps?

It's true that at the beginning I used to be ashamed to tell the truth and I used to hide it. I used to tell everyone that my father was dead and I was an orphan. But the psychologist told me that it wasn't nice to say that your father was dead when he wasn't, and she explained that I didn't have to be ashamed to tell the children the truth. So now I tell the truth, but nobody believes me any more, because I am Tilly Tall-Tale. What do I care if they don't believe me? At least they don't pester me all the time asking 'Where's your father?'

I couldn't care less. I hate them. I don't need them! I know children who have too much dad and mum at home. Their dad-mum nag them all day long and don't give them a moment's peace. So at least for me, this problem is solved.

For the meantime – anyway!

This passage poignantly illustrates the use of the defence mechanism of denial, erected not only against the divorce itself, but also against its direct and indirect consequences. In the escape from pain it is possible to discern signals of the distress which has arisen from the many losses. The danger of the girl and her mother exchanging roles, the girl becoming a 'parental child' may be discussed or role played in the group.

The following section of Tilly's story illustrates the use of humour for releasing mental distress.

Sometimes I long for my father, terribly. Ever since he left home and went abroad I miss him and I'm so very sad.

My mother Naomi has been left alone, that is with me, and with the smell of perfume that I'm not so mad about any more, and her beautiful clothes that she doesn't have anyone to wear them for. I often say to her: 'Mummy! Dress up nicely and go out and have a good time. Find yourself a boyfriend. Why are you sitting around the house so sadly, waiting for the telephone to ring? Only the old grandmothers call, and all the aunts with mustaches and long noses like trumpets come to visit us!' (This is what I say to her, but actually I won't agree to anyone taking my mother away from me!)

So she laughs and hugs me and I feel that she is also sad and that she is also longing, terribly, for my father.

My life's greatest dream is to bring my father back to live with my mother and with me and maybe I'd also get some more brothers and sisters from this. Because a woman who is alone cannot give birth. Babies are born only when there is a father at home who loves the mother and wants to have children. Children are born from love. And for love you need two. My mother explained all these things to me. I understand everything, except for the sentence: 'For love you need two.' 'Here I am, in love with H.I.Z. (These are his initials – when you love a boy you're supposed to write down only his initials!!) and he doesn't love me and doesn't want to be my boyfriend. So there aren't two persons in this love, are there? But I love him anyway – so is this love, or isn't it?

My mother calls this is one-sided love. What is 'one-sided love'? On one side there is someone who loves, and on the other side there is nobody.

This is only half a love, called, for short, 'onesidedlove.' I love H.I.Z. 'onesidedlove' and when I meet him in the street I have to write: 'I onesided him in the street!' This word has everything in it – how I am on the street, inside the one-side half. So it's no wonder he runs away, is it?

Children's Reactions

The stimulus for conversation is a story full of humour that makes many children burst out laughing on first hearing or reading it. This releases tension. When the tension dies down many emotional and painful subjects rise to the surface.

For instance:

Matthew: Mum went out with a boyfriend and left me with my elder
              sister. Her friend came and she went out too. I was so scared
              that I broke a window.

Zoe: When my mother went out with her boyfriend, I woke my
              little brother up and I went to a neighbour with him. When
              mum came home she was very angry.

Fiona: I am so scared of being alone that I switch on the TV set and
              jump under the blankets... When Mum comes back late at
              night she finds all the lights on, and me in bed. Before the
              divorce I wasn't afraid, even when I was alone.

Upon hearing Tilly Tall-Tale's words, 'My life's dream is to bring my father back
home to live with my mother and me...' Miriam said:

> Once it used to be hell at home – because of a secret I can't tell the group
> [*Miriam often kept secrets from members in the group*] and I phoned my dad
> to come... I didn't mean that he should come home to live, only that he
> should come and help us. Dad answered me over the phone: 'I can't come
> to you. I've got to stay with my little sons.' It's terribly annoying that he
> only cares for them – even when we are together.

The discussion may also turn to subjects such as Tilly's taking responsibility for
her mother.

Andrew: Our mother is like a prisoner. She only goes to work and back
              home. When she does go out, she just worries about us. We
              push her out of the house, telling her to have a good time.
              We don't like to see her at home – at home she is always sad.

Jane: Our Mum is mostly with us or with Martin, her friend.
              Sometimes they go out. We want her to go out very much,
              and we tell her so. But she also drives us out. She says 'Take
              some money and go and get yourselves some ice-cream!'

Alex: It helps me that I have older brothers, but I take responsibility
              for my mother ever since the divorce. I buy all sorts of things
              and help her so that she doesn't have to go out alone.

Children especially love the following excerpt from Tilly's story.

Practical Jokes

My mother has a doctor friend called Doctor Alfred Herbsett. He's called
Alfi for short, and he's not as stupid as he looks. (But he looks very, very
stupid!) When I hear him inviting my Mum to the movies, promising to
book tickets, I wait for my Mum to get out of the house, or to be busy

with something in another room, (as you know we have eight rooms in our house!) and I immediately dial his number:

'Doctor Herbsett!' he shouts loudly. (He's a little deaf.)

'Doctor!' I change my voice and say: 'This is Mrs. Kantzipolsky's daughter speaking...'

'Little girl!' he shouts. 'Tell your mother Kantzilposky that she is not my patient. Let her phone her own doctor!'

'But I can't speak to my mother Kantzipolsky!' I say.

'Why?'

'Because she has fainted. And the last thing she said to me before she fainted was your name!'

Alfi gets angry very quickly, but he is a good man. So he asks more quietly: 'Tell me, little girl, loudly please, what's wrong with your mother?' I answer, 'I don't know, Doctor. I don't think it is very serious, Doctor, only lots of froth is coming out of her mouth!'

'You don't understand a thing, child!' he says angrily. 'Isn't there any adult in the house?'

'No, there isn't!' I'm happy that I can tell him one true thing, 'My father left home and I live alone with my mummy.' And I begin crying.

'Where do you live?' he asks.

And I continue crying.

'Little girl!' he shouts. 'Where do you live?'

'At 3 Yehuda Raab Street in Petah Tikva.'

I see that he is beginning to hesitate.

'What, don't you have doctors in Petah Tikva?'

So I begin crying again and say: 'My mother said before she fainted...'

'Okay, okay, child,' he says, 'don't cry, I'm already on my way. What did you say your last name is?'

'Kantzipolsky, Techiyah Kantzipolsky! Thank you so very much. Al Al...' And here I almost gave myself away, because I almost called him Alfi, and only in the last minute did I say: 'Alfred Doctor Herbsett!'

'Alright, alright, child,' he takes pity on me. 'Try to remain calm and wipe the froth off your mother's lips.' And he puts the telephone down.

You can imagine the end. My mother waits and waits and Alfi doesn't come to take her to the movies. She phones him up and of course there is no answer. In the end he arrives at the very late hour, very angry and as red as a beetroot, and tell a story of running around for a long time in Petah Tikva looking for a street called Yehuda Raab, where there was a women who had fainted, that's what a little girl had informed him over the telephone, and in the end... no such thing to be found or heard of. People looked at him as though he were mad, for coming from Tel Aviv to Petah Tikva looking for a women called Techiyah Klatzipolsky (I almost correct him – Kantzipolsky!) Who doesn't exist at all at number three. Not in Yehuda Raab Street, and not in Moshe-Shmuel Raab and not in any other street in the vicinity.

My mother also looked at him as though he were mad, and told him that she hadn't expected such behaviour from someone as serious as him. He become even more upset and blushed. The movie tickets were lost, and he spoke loudly, as though he were deaf.

And he has never again been seen at our place with courtship and weddings on his mind. Only when Mum and I are sick we phone him and he comes, gives us a check-up, some medicine, laughs, blushes, has a cup of tea and goes away.

Sometimes I phone him, calling myself Techiya Kantzipolsky, and he shouts like a madman into the receiver.

Children's expressions of aggression towards the parents' new partners very often disrupt a family's rehabilitation. Reading the story and discussing and role-playing it can release the child from the burden of feelings of anger, guilt and fear of losing the remaining parent. The humour in the story enables a painful subject to be touched on without fear of hurting and releases and dissolves aggression safely.

Fears

Losing one parent by divorce inevitably raises the fear of losing the other. This fear is so fierce that it can hardly be approached directly. The book *Don't Throw Nani Out* (Zarchi 1979) tackles this issue on two levels. The overt level tells the story of two girls who find it difficult to accept Mother's new partner. The metaphoric level shifts the weight to the main character, a dog called Nani who becomes the centre of dramatic events. The conflicts in the family that this story exposes are dealt with in a group of children of divorce via dramatherapy.

Dramatherapy is a group process which explores, at many levels of metaphor, dramatic engagement between members. (Jennings, 1990) The following synopses of incidents from *Don't Throw Nani Out* serve as triggers for role-playing to expand the range of coping skills in the drama of divorce and remarriage.

Don't Throw Nani Out describes the relationships between Dori, her divorced parents and her stepmother. Dori finds it very difficult to accept the presence of a strange man in the house and is afraid that he can't stand her dog, Nani. This leads to her running away with Nani. Her mother and stepfather rush out looking for her, but in the meantime, Dori returns home and decides to hide in the attic, where she can hear the adults speaking. Nani makes a lot of trouble at home, eating socks and jumping up on the table. The relationship with the stepfather is full of tension: Dori neither accept nor trusts him. However, gradually the stranger gains her trust and even goes out for walks with the dog until one evening, when he and her mother go out for a walk with Nani – the dog manages to escape from the leash and a car runs her over.

Dori looks after her dog with the help of her stepfather, who goes to the vet with her and even holds Nani in his lap while she is being treated. This way he earns Dori's trust: When she is asked the name of the dog's owner – she gives her stepfather's name as well as her own.

Other themes in this story are suitable for bibliotherapy. One major theme is double loyalty: Dori is torn between being afraid that her father will be hurt if she doesn't stay for lunch, and being afraid that her mother will be angry if she doesn't come home on time. This raises many questions: What does Dori feel? What would you have felt in her place? What do you think of the solution Dori found?

There are many other issues raised here concerning children's responses following divorce – denial, running away, being ashamed in front of friends, taking revenge on the parents and testing their love, changing everyday habits, comparing parents' present situation to their pre-divorce state, and being incapable of accepting the finality of divorce.

Anger: When Darkness Becomes the Safest Thing in the World

The following are the thoughts of a boy whose parents' relationship is undergoing a crisis, on the eve of their separation. They are depicted in the book *Separation* by Amela Einat (1980). The first part of *Separation* is written as a personal diary by Ronen, a boy who sensitively describes his reactions to his parents' divorce. The second part of the book is an analysis of the main problems that face children when there is a crisis in the family and suggests how to provide a supportive attitude in similar situations.

> During the past few weeks I've felt as though it were winter at home, as though the words have frozen – nobody speaks any more. The worst is when everybody goes to bed and behind their bedroom door they begin arguing. Actually these are not arguments at all – you only hear her. I can't manage to understand what she is saying, but her voice sounds like crying. A sort of begging, which my father, the gentle one, doesn't seem to answer: That's the way it is every night. It's terribly difficult for me to listen, but it's as though some demon has got into me and doesn't let me fall asleep until it begins, and when it does begin, he pushes me into

listening more and more, until I get a stomach ache. Then I try to shut my ears with my hands and put my head under the pillow, and I want to escape – don't know where.

Sometimes I get scared of what I want to do to him.

Ronen hears his parents' quarrels from behind their locked door. He is aware of the anger which they are trying, in vain, to hide from him. At first nobody explains to him what the situation is, and he tries to understand what is happening with the help of bits of conversation that he overhears. This uncertainty undermines his self-confidence – at a time when he needs support and counselling very badly. He used to get it from his parents, but this is now impossible. He writes in his diary:

> To think that I was once afraid of the dark. To think that I once used to run to them when it thundered! What fun it was to be a baby. To believe they were big and strong, that by their side everything was safe, that they would solve all problems. How quickly you grow out of it. How the darkness become the safest thing in the world. When you don't see, don't hear, when you don't have to speak, when nobody nags you, when there's no school, no neighbors… Why are they doing this to me?

At school Ronen also feels a lack of self-confidence. He imagines that his teachers and friends know something. He seems to notice pity in his friends' eyes.

> This sweetness of theirs – they come to me during recess and ask me if I'd like to play football with them. When did they ever ask me before? They played, and that was that. I find it very difficult to succeed in school. Sometimes I don't exactly hear what is being said and I can't seem to concentrate during exams. Why are my parents doing this to me? Why are they making me feel so bad? As though I were a big zero in space. Why are they taking away the air I breathe, why are they killing everything for me? Maybe they don't know what to do themselves. Maybe they are punishing me and want me to be disappointed. Maybe I'm so bad that they are doing me a favour. Yes, I'm completely rotten and they're only doing me a favour.'

When Ronen's mother confirms his fears and tells him that things are not alright between her and his father ('Really, I must say this is news to me!' Ronen thinks sarcastically to himself), he runs away.

> That's it… I know it. All the time. I was scared to think about it… I knew that it was waiting for me. I shut my eyes and felt my heart emptying. I had such an emptiness inside. And the emptiness inside me hurt so much. and all the outside was one great confusion.

When confusion and embarrassment overcome him, following the news that his parents have indeed decided to separate, Ronen decides that he must do something to help himself. He makes himself a list of 'pros' and 'cons.' Pro: Mother will stop crying. Con: I'll be different from everybody else. I'm sure they'll all start talking about me and laughing at me. But the list leaves doubts in his heart and the list of questions becomes bigger than the lists of pros and cons. He is worried.

> How will I tell everybody? How will I part from Dad? Who will support us? Do people remain on non-speaking terms forever after divorce? Will Mum be able to manage? I can't lose her as well!

One morning everything becomes clear to him. He goes out for a walk with his mother. (She takes me out like a little puppy – for 'talking walks', he explains to the diary) when they suddenly see 'him' passing (the child has stopped calling him Dad) with a new girlfriend by his side.

> Mother squeezed my hand like a vice and whispered: 'Here she is, that slut. Do you see her, Ronen?' That's the way she spoke. 'Because of her he left us all.' And I had thought it was because of his university...

Is Ronen's suffering inevitable? How can it be ameliorated? It seems that the pains of separation and loss are inevitable and come in many different disguises. Uncertainty is one of the main sources of children's trauma. Quite often the divorcing parents are too preoccupied to notice their children's needs. At other times, the child may inadvertently become the scapegoat for parental frustrations.

Ronen's story is based on actual case material. Though his reactions to his parents' divorce are rather severe, they reflect the inner turmoil of many adolescents in similar circumstances. His story gives voice to their unspoken distress. It is meant to be read together by parents and children and may facilitate an open and healing communication between them.

Recommended books for children and adolescents experiencing divorce-related crises and tensions are listed in the Appendix. Some of the entries are annotated. This list is presently expanding, as is the use of bibliotherapy in schools and homes.

CHAPTER SEVEN

It is All in the Mind

The Power of Positive Thinking

In the beginning of this century a Swiss physician named Emil Coue (1922) found that it was possible to ameliorate pain and even recover from illness with the help of positive thinking. He recommended auto-suggestion, a method of self-brainwashing to improve health and enhance feeling of well being. The procedure seemed simple and consisted of endless repetitions of statements such as: 'Every day in every way I am getting better and better'. This idea that thought had the power to influence medical symptoms was met with scorn by scientists until recent scientific findings reconfirmed the claim (Pelletier 1987). Positive thinking is a conscious procedure of choosing to focus on benign elements of reality while disregarding the more obnoxious ones. People can regain self-confidence by convincing themselves of their merits. The popular notion of a 'self-fulfilling prophecy' has been validated by research (Rosenthal and Jacobson 1968). Another advocate of positive thinking ties its healing power to religious belief (Peale 1982). Our own research of coping styles among hostages has confirmed that faith can heal (Soskis and Ayalon 1986).

It is most important to consider the delicate balance between critical 'reality testing' and positive thinking, so as not to overlook certain negative aspects of the psychological defence mechanism of denial. It has also been asserted that moderate denial is beneficial to people caught up in stressful situations over which they have no control (Breznitz 1984). Denial can act as a means of self-protection. It is a way to pace gradual exposure to the stressful events or their meaning. It can protect individuals from becoming overwhelmed, providing them with the time needed to develop competent coping skills.

Stress Inoculation

The fact that divorced, one-parent families and blended families have become prevalent in our culture and no longer bear the stigma of social and psychological pathology sometimes blinds us to the burden of stress that these changes induce in the children's lives. Their distress is often experienced as victimisation, helplessness and a total loss of control.

Can this stress be mitigated?

The need and obligation to mitigate this stress and its ramifications has prompted us to develop a repertoire of stress-reduction activities, inspired by the methods of stress inoculation.

Meichenbaum (1983), quoting William James, maintains that 'the greatest revolution of our time is the discovery that human beings, by changing the inner attitudes of their minds, can change the outer aspects of their lives'. According to this optimistic point of view, stress is in the eye of the beholder'. 'It is not so much the event itself but our psychological perception of the implied threat that influences how we react. Individuals' perceptions, both of the stressfulness of the event and of their ability to cope with it ultimately define the stress' (p.22).

Even if they cannot change their external reality, children can be helped to transform their internal reality, the ways they think and feel, the way they perceive themselves, their parents, and interpret the events in their lives.

Inadequate coping strategies may lead to 'learned helplessness' (Seligman 1975). When children believe that they are unable to control or predict the occurrence of an aversive event, they lose self-confidence and trust in others and may be caught up in a vicious circle of self-defeating thoughts and behaviours.

There is a good deal of evidence that children, as well as adults, can turn 'learned helplessness' into resourcefulness by unlearning self defeating behaviours and diverting them into useful and positive channels. That this is a great challenge and a promising avenue has been explored further and validated by the practice and research of stress inoculation (Meichenbaum 1985). Stress inoculation is the psychological counterpart (or metaphor) of the more familiar procedure of biological immunisation against disease: like pathogens, stress is taken in small doses and antibodies are developed to combat and conquer it.

The key to successful coping is within the reach of those who acquire a repertoire of cognitive self statements and self-control skills and strategies, thus regaining mastery over their thoughts, feelings and actions. It is not a panacea, but helps to reduce distress to a manageable degree and turn stress into an opportunity to grow.

A children's verse sums it up quite succinctly:

> The little child who says 'I can!' will climb to the hill top.
> The little child who says 'I can't!' will at the bottom stop.

Interventions That Foster Self-Control Skills

The 'self-control' approach focuses on the teaching of personal and interpersonal attitudes and skills which the individual can apply to solve present and future psychological problems and to handle situations of stress more effectively. In this respect, the coping strategies and skills presented in these chapters, while designed for children of divorce, can be readily applied to any population to improve self-efficacy and inter-personal functioning. It is an approach that guides people towards improving their lives with the help of cognitive techniques such as decision making, self assertion or problem solving.

It is quite easy for a child, whose perceptions of reality is limited, to be caught up in a self-induced system of negative interpretations. Let us consider one five-year-old child's view of the events of parental separation. According to this scenario father has moved out of the family home and mother is struggling with her first salaried employment. This unprecedented situation gives rise to the child's fears of total abandonment. The child is unaware that her despair is evoked and maintained by an 'inner dialogue'. Within the therapeutic intervention she may be promoted to examine some 'self-statement such as: 'I am no good', 'nobody loves me' etc. Being helped to consider these as distorted misinterpretation of her external circumstances, she may be ready to try to change her 'self-talk' in a more constructive and positive light. While reality stays the same, the child's new perception of it makes it much more bearable.

Another child may believe in his power to affect a reconciliation between his parents and will go to extremes (falling severely ill, getting involved in accidents or breaking the law) trying to exercise this power. A reality-based examination of his inner dialogue may free him from this 'mission impossible' and enable him to address his grief and pain more directly.

Thus, interventions that foster self-control are designed to help children identify such dysfunctional cognitive patterns and generate alternative, more reality based, interpretations of a given situation. These skills require a lot of practice both through simulations and through actual life experiences. If the process is believable, safe and supportive, children may gain a great deal from it.

The purpose of the various strategies presented in our book is to supply parents and other helpers with a rich and multi-dimensional menu from which to choose those activities that are appropriate for children of assorted personalities, individual preferences, and who are experiencing different stages and severity of crisis.

It has become obvious by now that 'self-control' is not a single intervention but a composite of stress-reduction and prevention methods, all of which stem from a holistic approach to the interaction of all our faculties, mind, body and soul, and addresses it via many different channels.

The following chart attempts to classify those methods according to external, action oriented and internal, cognitively embedded interventions.

Self-Control

action-oriented

1. relaxation training
   * sharing feelings
   * receiving support
   * giving support

cognitive

2. guided imagery
3. inner dialogue
4. self-concept
5. assertive training

combined

6. problem solving

* represented throughout the book

---

1. Relaxation

Relaxation training is a self-control method. Evidence suggests that a substantial improvement will occur only when the individual realises that relaxation is an active coping skill to be practiced and applied to everyday life. One result is gaining increased control of one's reactions, for relaxation involves the individual's active participation in modifying responses to stressful life events. Like any other cognitive–behavioural skills which may be learned, relaxation requires practice.

Relaxation is achieved by loosening the tension of the exterior and interior muscles with the help of a set of directions. It occurs gradually, with changes in the breathing rhythm and by concentrating on parts of the body one at a time. It slows down the heartbeat and the electrochemical activity of the brain. Relaxation has proven necessary for the upkeep of both physical and psychological health. Relaxation may undo the damage caused by over stimulation and tension. There is a wide range of effects of relaxation that vary from person to person and even for each person from time to time. They have one main thing in common: the pleasant feeling they bestow. Relaxation is achieved by focusing attention without any voluntary effort and diverting attention from internal and external worries for a while.

Relaxation replenishes physical and spiritual energies. It is effective for reducing anxiety, pacifying rage, lengthening the attention span, and increasing learning ability. In times of crisis, especially in a prolonged life crisis, short periods of relaxation serve as 'time out' for restoring coping strengths. There are many methods for achieving relaxation of body and soul, where the contracted muscles are gradually relaxed, breathing becomes deep and rhythmic and attention is focused on breathing in and breathing out, enabling pleasant and peaceful scenes to be called to mind.

The following exercises combine movement and guided imagery (Ayalon 1978, 1992).

A JOURNEY THROUGH THE BODY

Materials: A tambourine or a small drum, a mat.

Set-up: A spacious room where participants can lie comfortably on their backs without feeling crowded. The atmosphere is calm and accepting.

Directions: The participants lie down on the mat on their backs. While they are loosening up and relaxing, they become aware of themselves and their bodies. They shut their eyes and listen to the rhythm of their breathing. If there are background noises, they listen and absorb them. Quietly and slowly the therapist's voice directs the gradual relaxation of every part of their bodies, from top to toe, or vice versa. Often a light touch helps the children relax.

Guided imagery follows:

We are about to embark on a journey inside the body. Choose any entrance and enter your body in your imagination. Now progress very slowly, feeling your way as you go along. Try and feel every muscle and bone. Move through the right arm, from the shoulder to the elbow, then to your palm and the fingertips. Do the same in your left arm. Go back to your chest, notice the pumping of your heart. Move carefully. Now to your stomach – make your own discoveries. Move all along your left leg, knee, ankle, foot and toes. Do the same in your right leg. Then come out of your toe and join us here.

The therapist can decide on the rhythm of the journey, varying it by lightly drumming. It is also possible to leave the choice of direction of the journey to the 'traveller'.

SWIMMING IN THE STORMY SEA

Make sure before starting that none of the participants has deep water anxiety. Then say softly:

You are swimming in the sea. Gradually it becomes stormy. The waves are rising, you are caught in a whirlpool... You strain with all your might, trying not to drown... You are very tired, almost desperate... But then you see a boat in the distance... Just a little more effort and... up you go! You've made it. You are saved. You are safely on board, breathing, panting, resting.

SENSORY RELAXATION TRAINING

Another effective method for relaxation that works well with children is approached indirectly. The children are told only to answer 'yes' or 'no' in their minds. (Lazarus 1978).

The therapist says the following, very slowly, to the children:

> Sit down comfortably in a chair so that your back and neck are adequately supported. You will be asked a series of questions. Each question can be answered 'yes' or 'no' but you do not have to answer the questions in this way. Simply test out your own particular reaction to each question. However you react is fine. There is no right or wrong way.

The following questions are then asked at five-second intervals.

- *Do you think you can feel pleasantly heavy?*

- *Are you able to be aware of your hands and arms?*

- *Can you feel that one of your arms is less relaxed than the other?*

- *Can you feel that one of your legs is more relaxed then the other?*

- *Do you think you can allow your eyes to close?*

- *Can you keep your eyes closed during the remainder of these questions?*

- *Can you imagine the distance from the top of your head to the point of your chin?*

- *Can you to imagine that you are looking at something that is far away?*

- *Can you feel the tension going away?*

- *Can you be aware of the space within your mouth?*

- *Can you picture a really peaceful scene? (ten-second pause)*

- *Can you feel a warm sensation somewhere in your body?*

- *Can you have calm and secure feelings? (ten-second pause)*

- *Can you allow your eyes to open?*

> If your eyes are not yet open, please open them now and allow yourself to feel awake and comfortable. How relaxed do you feel?

2. Guided Imagery

Day-dreaming and imagining are well-known human mental activities. We all imagine views, voices, movements, feelings, smells and tastes. These images have a great vitality, awakening deep emotional reactions, such as fear, excitement, sorrow and sexual stimulation, as well as many physical reactions which appear simultaneously, for example accelerated breathing and heartbeat, perspiration, muscular tension and widening of the pupils. This potential can be used to promote health and coping ability.

The invitation to engage in imagery comes from the therapist. The utterly relaxed participants receive cues and then freely complete the picture. The therapist directs the imagery according to the needs and aims of the therapy. With the help of imagery, it is possible to bring up subconscious feelings as well as to implant creative ideas. Images have psycho-physical influences and help recuperation from illnesses. An illuminating example is Simonton, Matthews-Simonton and Creighton's (1980) method of treating cancer: while relaxing, the patient evokes the following imagery: *'An army of white blood cells is flooding my veins, swallowing the cancer cells and destroying them'*. The patient repeats this imagery a few times a day, so that it turns into a healing power which reinforces the medical therapy.

The following exercise in guided imagery is effective in helping children relax.

A SAFE PLACE

> *Sit comfortably: legs apart, neither hand touching the other. Your eyes are getting heavier. Now they are closing. Breathe deeply, be aware of your breathing. Feel how your feet are turning into balloons. Your head and other parts of your body are turning into balloons as well. Now prick the balloons with a pin and let all the air out. You are calm and relaxed... In your imagination my words will take you on a journey. Just listen to my voice. Find a pleasant place, a place where you feel safe, protected and loved and where you feel you belong. You feel good in this place. It can be a place where you felt good in the past, or in the present. If you can't find a place like this, imagine such a place for yourself. Stay in this place... Who do you see there? What do you feel? What gives you strength? Now, in your imagination, go over to an unpleasant place, a place where you feel strange, ostracised, different, lacking in self-confidence. Where is this place? Who is there? How do you react? Stay in this place as long as you can stand it. Then, at your own pace, go over to the former place, the safe place.*

> *Very slowly, return here. You may open your eyes and look around you. Without a word, write down what you have just experienced. Draw, act or tell one another about your experience.*

> *From now on, whenever you are in distress or feel the need, you can return to your good and safe place and draw strength from it.*

3. Modifying the Inner Dialogue

The silent conversation that eternally takes place between us and ourselves is directly responsible for the way we feel and act.

Ellis (1991) uses a five-step model to describe the relation between the external and the internal reality. According to him it is not the event (**A**) but our interpretation of it to ourselves **(B)** that makes us feel and behave in a certain way **(C)**.

(A) Activating Event ⸻ **(B)** Beliefs ⸻ **(C)** Consequences.

(B) is the arena of the inner dialogue, where a lot of misinterpretations and irrational thinking, of which we are usually unaware, take place.

The therapist helps the participants to follow the inner thread of thoughts and expectations, that transmit painful feeling such as fear, humiliation, surrender or submission. They gradually learn to modify the exaggerated and distorted reactions by replacing self-defeating statements with more rational, benign ones, advancing two more steps:

(D) Dispute, Debate, Discriminate and Define – the individual tries to find evidence, seeks alternate explanations and clearer definitions. This self-talk is designed to dispute and modify the irrational beliefs.

(E) Refers to the individual's new Effect or philosophy, which helps him think more rationally and constructively.

The following are examples of inner dialogue marked by irrational statements:

- Why it is always me they pick on? (*anger*)
- What did I do to make father leave us? (*guilt*)
- There is nothing left for me to do but cry. (*helplessness*)
- If you could hurt me like this, then I'll hurt you. (*revenge*)

MODIFICATION (REFLECT AND SHARE)

(A) In what situations are you most upset, angry, frustrated, nervous?

(B) What do you usually say to yourself at such times?

(C) How does this 'self-talk' affect your behaviour?

(D) Find more rational statements and try them to see which fits you best.

(E) Repeat your new 'self-talk' to the group, until you feel comfortable with it and can act on it.

USEFUL STATEMENTS FOR INNER DIALOGUE

Meichenbaum (1984) suggests a training format for general facilitative statements, progressing step by step:

1. Preparation
2. Confrontation

3. Coping

4. Reinforcement.

These statements are tailored for each individual case, to be practiced and rehearsed.

The following examples of statements useful at each stage of the inner dialogue can be adapted, rehearsed and used.

4. Feeling Good About Oneself

Self-concept is a set of perceived traits and values that people attribute to themselves and then behave accordingly. It is built early in childhood and is composed of expectations that people have of themselves. It can easily misinterpret reality to the degree that even success would be experienced as failure. People with positive self-concepts trust themselves and dare to try out new things. People with negative self-concepts tend to abstain from coping, avoid effort and lack initiative. Information that comes through the senses will often be blocked, distorted, limited or wrongly interpreted. The self-concept is highly resistant to change. Changing it takes more than just positive thinking. In fact, a negative self-concept actively impedes positive thinking. A basic part of acquiring coping skills is building a positive self-image, supported by acceptance of others and enhanced by positive body awareness.

5. Becoming Assertive

Assertiveness means knowing your rights, sticking to your opinions and expressing your needs clearly and forcefully without hurting others. Assertive communication is built on respect for yourself and others, leaving place for compromise when there are conflicting demands. It is important to remember that assertive behaviour is not always a guarantee for success in achieving a purpose (Keat 1979).

Useful Statements for Inner Dialogue

	If you are angry...	*If you are afraid...*
P R E P A R I N G	I have to know what makes me angry, to find out when I begin to to be furious.	I have to get to know what makes me afraid.
	What should I do?	What can I do so that this won't won't happen?
	I shouldn't take it to heart.	Who could help me?
	I musn't be hurt so quickly.	With whom can I talk? Who should I phone?
	I must remember my plan of action.	When I am afraid, I must remember what I have to do.
C O N F R O N T I N G	Breathe deeply; practice relaxation exercises.	Breathe deeply; calm down slowly but surely.
	It's not worth getting angry.	I won't sink into my fear; instead I'll think of what to do.
	I can control the situation.	I can remember how I overcame fear last time.
	It's difficult, but I can overcome my anger.	I can deal with it. It will pass, soon.

Useful Statements for Inner Dialogue (continued)

<table>
<tr><td rowspan="5">C
O
P
I
N
G</td><td>The more I remain calm, the better I can control the situation.</td><td>The fear I feel is a sign that I should continue with relaxation exercises.</td></tr>
<tr><td>I can think of ways to handle this!</td><td>I'll find out what is really happening.</td></tr>
<tr><td>I won't be swept along by this provocation.</td><td>I'll grade the intensity of my fear on a scale of 0–10.</td></tr>
<tr><td>They won't make me mad!</td><td rowspan="2">It's natural to be afraid in this situation; but I will figure out what to do instead of being afraid.</td></tr>
<tr><td>I know how to manage; if not now, then later on.</td></tr>
</table>

Reinforcing Statements

It worked! I did it!

It wasn't as hard as it seemed!

The fear seemed much worse than it really was.

I knew I would cope!

How will my parent/teacher react when I tell her/him about this?

When I control these ideas, I also control my fears/anger.

I am pleased with my improvement.

An assertive approach is of great importance to children who are trying to manoeuvre their way through the crisis of divorce. Assertiveness training teaches them to distinguish between inefficient reactions of aggressiveness or self-depreciation and efficient reactions of taking a stand and expressing it clearly, without blaming and without feeling guilty.

The goal of assertiveness training is to deal with the various conditions characteristic of stress in an effective manner. It is therefore important to provide concrete examples of the differences between non-assertiveness, aggression and assertive behaviour.

To the participants:

If in conflict, in need, or facing an unacceptable demand

DON'T *plead, placate, withdraw, submit.*

DON'T *attack, fight, push, shout, insult.*

Do *state your needs, beliefs or rights – clearly and firmly.*

Do *learn to say 'no' in a convincing way. (In the group setting, rehearse various ways of saying 'no').*

Do *repeat your statement calmly and confidently, until you are heard.*

It is OK to ask for what you want, even if you don't always get it.

Assertiveness is best practiced within the group. The training aims to eliminate cognitive or emotional obstacles that disturb the use of assertiveness – such as feelings of guilt, anger, anxiety or irrational thinking.

To distinguish between their own rights and the rights of others, children learn the difference between 'I' sentences and 'you' sentences. The following activities are introduced as practice for developing this assertive attitude. Each activity presents a dilemma through which the child is guided to practice assertive behaviour in three phases:

(a) understanding of the other person(s) involved;

(b) expressing the child's own feelings in a clear and straightforward way;

(c) suggesting various other solutions.

6. The Challenge of Solving Problems

When a problem seems complicated and threatening, the proven technique of 'problem solving' enables lessening of the threat and heightening of the efficiency of coping (Wheeler and Janis 1980). The problem solving approach teaches the child to stand back and systematically analyse a problem situation in the absence of any acute stress. This coping skill approach concentrates on teaching the child how to identify problems, generate alternative solutions, tentatively select a solution, and test and verify the efficacy of that solution in real-life conditions.

The major advantage of group counselling in the 'problem solving' approach is that more sources of knowledge and information regarding alternatives and consequences are available, thus providing a more adequate 'model' for problem solving. In addition, group discussion may encourage a more adequate appraisal of alternatives and, as a result, increase the effectiveness of decision-making. Interpersonal interactions and social reinforcement facilitate application of the technique to real-life social situations. The procedure to be followed is:

(a) Identify the problem and define it in clear, specific terms (it is advisable to do it in writing).

(b) Imagine as many probable and varied solutions as possible – 'brainstorming'. These ideas are put into a 'solution pool'.

(c) Make a list of 'gains' and 'losses' (or 'pros' and 'cons') for every one of the proposed solutions.

(d) Place the solutions in hierarchical order based on the apparent difficulty in reaching them. It is worth remembering that every problem has more than one solution!

(e) Try to implement the best solution. If that is impossible, choose the next best one and so on. It is advisable to role-play the problems and their solutions before trying them out in real-life.

Even though these steps seem reasonable, they are very rarely applied in stressful situations. To turn them into a positive and constructive habit, it is worth practicing them repeatedly.

What can facilitate problem solving?

- Dividing the problem into 'little portions' and dealing with each part separately
- Distinguishing between what is possible to change and what is not
- Accepting that which is impossible to change
- Asking for advice and counselling
- Not getting discouraged by failures. A failure can be an opportunity to try out a new way.

HOW THE THERAPIST CAN HELP CHILDREN DEVELOP PROBLEM-SOLVING SKILLS

The participants are asked to list a series of problem situations. These are placed in hierarchical order based on the apparent level of difficulty in reaching a solution. Training should begin with the least difficult and progress toward the more difficult categories. The counsellor helps to:

(a) Construct a specific problematic (hypothetical or actual) situation.

(b) Guide the participants towards a definition of the problem in clear, specific terms.

(c) Formulate the target objectives for problem-solving in clear statements, describing those aspects of the problematic situation that are to be changed, and the exact nature of the changes.

The next step is to elicit a range of possible solutions among which the effective ones for dealing with the particular problem may be found. One possible method is through 'brainstorming'.

The following guidelines can be useful:

(a) All criticism is ruled out. Ideas are not evaluated at this stage.

(b) Encourage children to come up with ideas regardless of their value, acceptability or appropriateness.

(c) Many ideas are required. The larger the number of ideas, the greater the likelihood of finding some useful ones among them.

(d) Cross-fertilisation and development of ideas. Participants should indicate how the ideas of others can be improved or how two or more ideas can be developed into yet another idea.

These criteria are followed in order to prevent the premature termination of the problem solving process. They provide the initiative to maintain the search even after the first 'good' alternative is suggested. Likewise, they are designed to prevent abandonment of the search because of an early series of 'poor' ideas.

In evaluating the ideas, attention needs to be paid to the likely consequences of each course of action, and an examination made of the usefulness of these consequences in resolving the problem. In selecting the most appropriate strategy, attention is focused on general courses of action likely to resolve the major issues, However, in selecting the most appropriate tactic, the focus is on the likelihood of being able to completely implement the strategy.

Children are told to ask themselves: 'If I were to carry out this particular solution, what are the various things that could possibly happen as a result?' To help them in this process, they are instructed to consider the consequences in four different categories: personal, social, short-term and long-term.

The children are then asked to consider the value (positive – negative – neutral, or satisfactory – unsatisfactory – neutral), and the likelihood that each of these three consequences will occur. At this point, participants can judge the various alternatives, considering the consequences of each, according to their values and likelihood of occurrence. Thus, they are able to select the one alternative which seems to have the best chance of solving the problem satisfactorily, while maximising the likelihood of positive consequences and minimising the likelihood of negative ones.

Children are instructed to verify the solution by observing an action's various consequences in the real life situations and by comparing these outcomes with the outcome predicted when the decision was made. If the comparison is unsatisfactory, the child returns to the decision-making phase of the strategy and selects the 'second-best' alternative for action. He repeats this procedure until a satisfactory outcome is achieved, at which point the solution is verified and the process is completed.

EXPLAINING THE RULES OF THE GAME

(a) Divide the group into working pairs.

(b) Each pair gets a card.

(c) Each pair thinks of a solution to their problem, and then describes the solution to the group.

(d) Members of the group get a chance to relate to the proposed solution and to add ideas of their own.

(e) Pairs can exchange cards.

(f) The children role-play one chosen situation, exchanging roles of the 'helper' and the 'helped'.

EXAMPLES OF QUESTIONS POSED IN PROBLEM-SOLVING CARDS

- Ever since your parents told you about the divorce, your younger brother Richard has been crying in school. His teacher asks you to help him stop crying.
  What do you do?

- Your big brother has moved in with Dad. Your Mum asks you to persuade him to return.
  What will you do?

- You are in bed and you overhear your parents fighting – they seem to be arguing over 'the children'.
  What can you do about it?

- You are ill at home. Dad arrives to visit and you begin playing a board-game together.
  Suddenly Mum interferes and says angrily: 'That's the game *I* bought you for Christmas. Your father has no business playing it with you'.
  What will you do?

Simon Learns Self-Control Skills – A Case Study

Simon, aged twelve, came for consultation six months after his parents' divorce. The referral note explained that his symptoms consisted of depression, feelings of helplessness and suicidal thoughts. Ever since the divorce he had been suffering from headaches and pain in his chest. The interview revealed a lot of repressed anger. Therapy was applied in three stages, teaching self-control strategies.

Stage A: Recognizing Anger and Giving Permission to Talk About it Openly

Simon learned to identify people and situations that caused him anger, and to spot within himself signs and signals that heralded this reaction. This enabled him to avoid, as much as possible, distressing situations and to reduce tension at the very beginning. He learned to distinguish between justified anger and anger that was caused by fears and defensiveness.

Stage B: Learning and Training of Coping Skills

Simon practiced rehearsing situations as problems that had solutions, instead of looking at them as threats that endangered his safety. He defined his immediate aims and prepared a list of the best ways to achieve them. Therapy consisted of relaxation, humour and the release of stress.

Stage C: Desensitisation of Anger Reactions

This was done by gradual exposure to small doses of annoying stimuli, through guided fantasy and role playing. Later, Simon was asked to imagine scenes from his day-to-day life and to grade them according to the intensity of anger they aroused in him, beginning with the least annoying and going up to the enraging ones. These situations were also brought to life by role playing. Towards the end of his therapy, Simon started applying the coping skills he had learned to real life situations, beginning with rather easy situations, and moving on to more difficult ones. Eventually, he was relieved from depression, succeeded to remain calm most of the time and could express his feelings more effectively and openly.

PART IV

SUPPORT GROUPS FOR CHILDREN

CHAPTER EIGHT

Starting a Group

Man wishes to be confirmed in his being by man, and wishes to have a presence in the being of the other. Secretly and bashfully he watches for a Yes which allows him to be, and which can come only from one human person to another. (Buber 1965)

Shared Experience

Children learn about themselves by comparing themselves to others. The figure that is reflected to the child in the 'social mirror' turns into the basis on which he or she can build a self-concept. A positive experience of belonging and mutuality in a group gives children many valuable opportunities for changing the low self-esteem that has developed in the 'distorted mirror' of their traumatic life experiences. That is why these groups are of such great value as a support system.

The small group – the family – is the basic social system into which human beings are born and in which they become people. In this system we shape our personalities and our capacities for developing intimacy, empathy and mutual caring. Later on, the peers (classmates and neighbourhood friends) become the meaningful figures with whom we interact and develop. Promising a child a place in a group, even if the initiative comes from outside, saves the child from loneliness.

The warm relationship that is built up in the support group – intimacy, attention, encouragement and support – gives its members a feeling of security and belonging. These feelings give individuals the strength to share their emotions, thoughts and ideas with the others. The small number of participants (as opposed to the number of pupils in class, for instance) enables each one to express her- or himself, to gain attention, to be responded to, and to have a sense of belonging.

The small group is most suitable for tasks connected with emotional learning, and for counselling, therapy and development of skills for coping with threatening situations. It allows children to express feelings of anger and fear without having to be afraid of censure or criticism. Each of the participants has a unique story concerning divorce-related complications that have arisen in his or her life. While listening to the other members' personal stories, the participants realise that they are not crippled or different from others. They measure the normality of their reactions against those of their friends in the group and gradually develop a sense of self-esteem. Hearing others speak of experiences similar to their own is very often exactly the boost the child needs. It is also proof that it is possible to overcome difficulties. These factors are more important than the encouragement of people who are outside the circle of divorce (Hammond 1981).

In addition, researchers and practitioners have responded to the need for intervention with families experiencing divorce by introducing the children to groups, because they are considered to be an effective and cost-efficient method of enhancing positive adjustment outcomes (Pfeifer and Abrams 1984, Sonnerstein-Schreider and Baird 1986).

Gwynn and Brantley (1987) report improvement in children's self-concept and adaptive social skills following participation in intervention groups, as well as reduced behavioural problems (e.g. acting out) and increased competencies such as assertiveness and appropriate school behaviour. Furthermore, after intervention with five groups of six children, each over an eight week period, these researchers found that depression, anxiety and negative feelings about divorce decreased, and interaction in the treatment group increased.

Participation in group counselling sessions has also proved to be very effective in achieving an inner locus of control among young adolescents from divorced families (Omizo and Omizo 1988). In turn, with the help of group-leaders, young adolescents have served as important normalising developmental facilitators for children undergoing divorce (Lesowitz et al. 1987).

Another advantage of meetings among children with 'shared experience' lies in the fact that the members of the group are in different stages of their adjustment to divorce. There are some in the first stage of their family's dissolution, and others who are undergoing the tension of waiting for a judge's custody ruling. Others are confused over their feelings concerning a parent's new partner, while others still are already coping with the complications of a blended family and are searching for their places in the maze of relationships with a stepfather or mother, his or her children, and the new children born to a remarried parent. (The fact that there are no real names for the kinship relationships that follow divorces complicates communication on these subjects, as well as the ability to find new patterns of suitable behaviour.) The participants reflect varied experiences in a wide range of divorce-situations, providing an opportunity to look intently at the divorce procedure in a very tangible way, and to find suitable behavioural, emotional and cognitive responses.

The small group is a most efficient setting in which to develop resolutions to problems. In a supportive and helpful atmosphere, it is possible to bring up questions for discussion, to role-play new behaviours, to learn coping techniques in simulation games, to mutually counsel and be counselled. In a group that nurtures mutuality and multi-directional communication, the participants are released from inhibitions, shame and hesitation, and are motivated to participate in the activities. When youngsters come to believe that their contribution to the group is meaningful, their involvement in group assignments is enhanced.

Creating the Group

It is a good idea to limit the number of participants in a group to between seven and fifteen (Yalom 1985). Furthermore, the group should include, in balanced numbers, children undergoing various stages of the divorce process. The temptation to offer group support only to youngsters in early or acute phases of divorce should be resisted; children with longer experience may also need such support and, in addition, can contribute valuable insights and describe efficient ways of coping. An optimal combination of small group size and diversity makes both group activities and individual self-expression possible within the time available.

There are a number of ways in which suitable candidates are directed to the groups:

1. Referrals by teachers, who have identified great changes in the child's study performance, behaviour, or social life;

2. Referrals by parents, who ask for help for their children during the family crisis;

3. Application by children themselves who, encouraged by other children or by classroom contact with the counsellor, have become aware that there is someone to turn to.

The following incident illustrates the above:

> In a meeting with children in the fourth grade, the counsellor illustrated the use of 'TA for Children' (see Chapter 14). Standing in front of the class she showed the children a Russian doll in the shape of a tea cosy. Under her wide skirt were three dolls that symbolized the three ego-states: 'child', 'adult' and 'parent'. With the help of the dolls the children learned to distinguish between suitable and unsuitable ways of resolving

classroom quarrels. After the lesson, one of the boys in the class approached the counsellor, telling her his story:

'My father doesn't behave like an "adult". I think the "child" in him has overcome the "adult" and it's a "bad child", which is very frightening.'

After describing the father's cycle of aggression towards the boy and his mother followed by great remorse, 'also like the "child"', as the boy declared, the student was invited to join a group for children of divorced parents (after receiving permission from his estranged parents). The following day he brought another boy with him:

'He also has a similar problem. I told him that he should speak about it in the group!'

It is necessary to receive the parents' permission, both verbally and in writing, before including a child in the group counselling process. A personal conversation with each candidate, to discuss the aims of group meetings and to determine whether the youngster is motivated to participate, is also a prerequisite.

Rules for Group Activities

It is important for the group to build basic rules of interpersonal communication that include the following:

- Members will listen to one another without judgement or criticism
- Each member has the right to speak; no one is permitted to dominate discussions
- Members will relate to one another and give each other feedback
- The group will maintain an atmosphere of tolerance and mutual respect
- Personal stories are to be kept secret.

In each meeting a transition from the demanding atmosphere of school to the releasing atmosphere of the group takes place. These transitions are necessary to create willingness for free self-expression and for giving and receiving support, as well as for change.

The facilitator helps the transition along by using a number of 'warm-up' activities, geared to three goals:

1. Building trust in the therapist.

2. Developing trust and communication among the children.

3. Creating a 'conflict-free zone' in which creative activities can take place. These activities have a twofold purpose: relaxing diversion, and the search for alternative solutions for distressing situations.

Music, games and relaxation exercises, comfortable chairs and some light refreshments help create the appropriate ambience.

Beginning: Step by Step

The three initial stages creating a group are:

1. Deciding on 'the rules of the game' or the 'contract'.

2. Getting acquainted (on two planes: getting to know oneself and getting to know each other).

3. Developing a vocabulary for expressing feelings.

The Contract

The early establishment of group structures and rules, especially with children in the latency period (roughly ages 6–12) who have boundless energy and are likely to disrupt the sessions, is very important. With the help of the rules, which form a tightly focused structure (rather than the freewheeling chaos typical of children's groupings), children learn and interact, allowing group cohesion and commitment to develop quickly. The rules of the 'contract' are different from one group to another. They are usually decided upon by the group after the therapist, in a modelling role, has made initial suggestions (although, in some cases, the therapist establishes most of the rules).

Useful rules include the following:

- We'll accept each person the way he or she is. We'll respect each other and we won't judge one another.
- We'll speak about ourselves in the first person.
- If someone wants to remark or comment about something another member has said or done in the group, he or she will address the other direct rather than discussing the matter in the third person.
- There won't be any conversation or secrets between two members in the group while a third is speaking or a discussion is taking place. Everyone listens to the person speaking.
- A member may not choose to 'not be on speaking terms' with another participant. It is alright to be angry at another, but it is preferable to express this anger verbally.
- Anything said in the group is confidential. It is against the rules to turn children's feelings or thoughts into weapons against them or to gossip about them.
- No-one will be forced to speak. Children who sit quietly in the group may also be emotionally involved, enjoying themselves and learning from others' stories.

After rules have been proposed, the group discusses, amends, selects, and accepts them, sometimes even setting them down in a charter which each member signs.

Getting Acquainted: The Legend of My Birth and Name

These instructions are given in a quiet voice, very slowly. Allow time for imagination. The personal stories may be written or drawn before being told to the other members of the group.

> *Please close your eyes.*
>
> *In your imagination, return to the day of your birth. Try and see your family on this very special day. How does your mother look? How does your father look? Were there any more brothers or sisters in your family? As far as you know, were they expecting a boy or a girl? Who else was waiting for you to be born (uncles and aunts, grandfathers and grandmothers, friends)?*
>
> *Which name was chosen for you? Who chose this name? How did they decide upon this choice? Were you named after anyone? Who? What do you know about this person? Have you ever tried to be like this person?*
>
> *What were your pet names in the family? What pet names or nicknames do your friends have for you? Do you like your name? What does it mean to you? Would you have liked to be called something else?*
>
> *What would you like to be called in this group?*

Miriam's parents were divorced after her father had become a paraplegic following an accident in the army. Although she had joined the group on the condition that she wouldn't have to speak at all, she rushed to be the first to tell her story:

> Both my parents gave me my name when I was born. I was so happy then, because I didn't know that my life would be a disaster and that I'd have to live with grandma and grandpa and that my brother and sister would be thrown into an institution!

This exercise blends 'the beginning of life' and the building of the family. With the birth of each child, a family changes its composition and all its interrelationships. It is worth stressing the fact that the children have spent some good times with their families: times of growth, expansion and pleasure. Even if the family has broken up, the moment of birth is very often symbolised by the acceptance and happiness that were once a part of the children's lives.

Nevertheless, some participants may be very vulnerable and sensitive to activities concerning family memories. These children must receive a lot of support during the getting-acquainted process.

Developing a 'Feelings Vocabulary'

To participate fully and effectively in the group, children need a rich and precise vocabulary to describe their feelings. This idea can by introduced by presenting the following metaphor (Snunit 1984):

The Soul Bird

Deep down, inside our bodies, lives the Soul.
No one has ever seen it,
But we all know it's there.
Not only do we know it's there,
We know what's in it, too.

Inside the Soul
Right in the middle of it,
There's a bird standing on one foot.
This is the Soul Bird.

It feels everything that we feel:

When somebody hurts our feelings, the Soul
Runs Round and round in pain.

When someone loves us,
It hops and skips
Up and down,
Backwards and forwards.

When someone calls our name,
It listens carefully

To hear what kind of call it is.
When someone is angry with us,
It curls itself into a ball
And is silent and sad.
And when someone hugs us, the Soul Bird,
Deep down inside,
Grows and grows
Until it almost fills us.
That's how good it feels when someone hugs us.

Deep down, inside, lives the Soul.
No one has ever seen it,
But we all know it's there.
Never, never has a person been born
Without a Soul.
It sparks the moment we are born
And never leaves us.

Not even once,
For as long as we live.
It's like the air that people breathe
From the moment they are born
Until the time they die.

Do you want to know what the Soul Bird is made of?
Well, it's really quite simple:
It's made of drawers.
These drawers can't be opened 'just like that',
Because each is locked with its own special key!
Only the Soul Bird can open its drawers.

How?

Ah, that's quite simple too:
With its other foot!

The Soul Bird stands on one foot,
And with its other foot (tucked under its wing when it's resting)
It turns the key to the drawer it wants to open,
Pulls the handle, and lets everything inside – out!

Because there is a drawer for everything we feel,
The Soul Bird has many, many drawers:
One for being happy and one for being sad;
One for being jealous and one for being content;
One for being hopeful and one for despair;
One for being patient and one labeled 'I can't wait!';
There is also one for hating
And one for being loved.
There is even a drawer for being lazy and one for being vain.
And there is a special drawer
Hardly ever opened
For your deepest secrets.

There are other drawers too –
Whatever drawers you dream of.

The therapist then asks the children to draw the Soul Bird, (for very young children it may be a good idea to draw one in advance) and to draw two drawers of any shape they wish. One is a drawer full of secrets and the other is a drawer for feelings. Next, the children should draw keys to fit each drawer and consider their shape, what they're made of, and what would help these keys to open their very own drawers (Lahad and Ayalon 1993).

> 'My fear drawer is so full it's bursting, so that any key with love and understanding, and a promise not to tell anyone, will open it,' said John at the session.

> 'Maybe the code to open my "secrets" drawer is this group,' said Rachel. 'I know they care about me, will keep my secrets and not tell anyone.'

The children understand the message of this activity very well, and refer often to their cherished soul-bird and to the drawers opening up in the group.

> Eight-year-old Tom was very restless during one of the group sessions, and disturbed the activities. He twiddled around with his shoes and his scarf and jumped up and down in his chair. When prodded to explain what the matter was, he said:

> 'You're not helping me open the drawer full of secrets or the excitement drawer. The key that would help them open up is attention. You see, Dad was let out of prison yesterday and came to visit me. He bought me these new shoes and this scarf.'

This was the first inkling the group had of Tom's father having served a term in prison and of his feelings about the burden he was bearing in addition to the divorce.

The Group Process

The chart on the following page suggests how a group's time might be divided and used during a school year. It goes without saying that the entire process must be carried out with love, caring, support and empathy.

The Group Process
(suggested allocation of time)

←——— *Total Time* ———		*The School Year* ————————→	
25% *(5–6 meetings)*	*1* *meeting*	50% *(minimum of 10–12* *meetings)*	25% *(3–4 meetings)*
Opening		*Group* *Development* *Therapy*	*Closure*
Introductions		Expressive therapies	Partings
Ice-breakers		Inoculation	Endings
	C		
Warm-ups		Developing assertiveness	
	R		Feedback
Legend of name	I	Understanding ego-states (transactional analysis)	Party
Building 'feelings	S	Bibliotherapy	
vocabulary'	I	Developing responsibility	
Constructing rules	S	Locus of control	
		Values clarification	
The contract			
Building trust			

CHAPTER NINE

Building Trust

Getting to Know Each Other

Because we believe that participating in groups should be enjoyable for these children, who, in their new circumstances, have few opportunities for pleasure, we start the group sessions with warm-up activities. The counsellor or therapist should prepare a varied list of such activities, so that he or she can begin the sessions and help the children to get going. These can be physical/verbal activities or simple drama or painting activities. Any activity that helps the children make meaningful contact with each other helps (Liebmann 1986, Jennings 1986). Here are a few ideas to introduce the children to each other and to group activities, and to help them 'thaw':

I Am and I Like...

The first person says her name, adding something that symbolises her (or something that she hates, loves, loves to eat, or an animal). The next person then says the first one's name and choice and adds his own; the third person repeats both former statements and names, adding her own, and so on. This is a good activity for the very beginning of the group, as it helps to teach the children to look into each others' eyes when they talk and to speak directly to the other participants, for example, 'Your name is Tom and you like carrots, my name is Lynn and I like chocolate'.

Bean-Bag

Two participants throw a ball or bean-bag from one to the other, with the catcher calling out the name of the thrower.

Personal 'Gifts'

Each participant introduces herself and states what she will offer the group. This 'contribution' must begin with the first letter of her name, for example, 'My name is Tania and I will add truthfulness to the group'... 'My name is Oliver and I will add openness to the group'... 'My name is Louise and I will add love to the group'.

Copy-Cat

Each participant announces his name and accompanies it with a movement. The whole group repeats the name and movement, and announce themselves one by one, repeating all the names and movements serially.

Mimed Introductions

Each child introduces herself by miming something characteristic of her nature, or something she loves; the others try to guess what it is.

Group and Regroup

The leader calls out different ways of grouping, for example, all those with brothers/sisters, blue/brown eyes, who hate/love spinach, live with mother/father etc.

How About That!

The group breaks up into small groups of four or five. Each subgroup makes a list of all the things its members have in common, including characteristics. The list can be discussed when the whole group reassembles. It is also possible to make this activity competitive (*'Let's see which group finds the most things'*.)

Circles and Lines

With (or without) musical accompaniment, the children are asked to walk briskly around the room and, when given a signal, *freeze*. The next instruction is to walk in straight lines only (making 90° or 180° turns)... *and freeze*. The next instruction can be to walk in curved lines only, skirting others smoothly... *and freeze*.

Colour Touch

The leader calls out two colours. The children have to touch one on themselves and one on someone else. For example, if 'black and green' are called, the child touches his own black hair and his friend's green sweater.

Body Touch

The leader calls out two parts of the body. (for example, elbow/shoulder) and then explains that *'your elbow touches another child's shoulder'*. The whole group does this exercise simultaneously.

Zoom!

In turn, each child has just one minute in which to touch the four corners of the room, the floor, two chairs and five pairs of knees. They must then retrace their steps exactly. Can the participants remember whose knees they touched, and in what order?

Telephone Foibles

The children sit in a circle and the first one whispers a word which the others pass along. The last one says the word aloud and it is compared to the original.

Backboard

The children sit in a circle, each facing the next person's back. The first person passes a short word on by 'writing' it (with a finger) on the next person's back. When it has gone round the circle, the final word is compared with the original.

Pass the Mask

The children sit in a circle. The first person pulls a face, then with his hands 'passes' the mask to the next person, who puts it on (imitates it), develops it into a new mask, and then passes it on.

Mirroring

In pairs, one person mirrors the other's actions. They then switch roles and repeat the game.

Getting the Group Started

Everyone in turn says a few words or a sentence beginning:

> On the way to school I noticed...
>
> A special feeling I've had this week is...
>
> Something I am excited about is...
>
> What I expect from this group is...
>
> Right now I'm feeling...

The Language of the Heart

Children need to enrich their 'feelings vocabulary' in order to express their emotions accurately. It is necessary to help them identify the spectrum of feelings connected with different behaviours and social situations. Through actions, tasks, exercises and games they can learn of 'body language', the language of facial expressions and their varied meanings. Awareness and perception of intrapsychic feelings are thus achieved.

The following are a few activities which develop awareness and help build a vocabulary for defining and identifying feelings.

The 'Feelings Wheel'

The Feelings Wheel is a very efficient way of learning the vocabulary of feelings. The wheel arouses motivation for participation in the group: it passes from hand to hand, with each participant spinning it like a roulette wheel until it comes to a stop at one of the feelings named on the wheel. The participant calls to mind some incident where he or she has experienced this feeling. The group leader then develops these themes, encouraging discussions and role-playing.

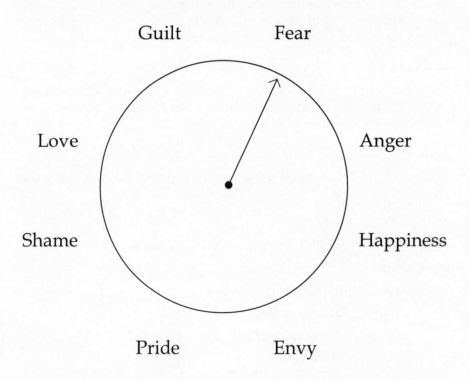

Figure 9.1: The 'Feelings Wheel'

The following examples occurred in a group of nine-year-olds:

Happiness: I am happy that my parents got divorced... now I don't have to listen to her cursing him.

Hate: I hate my dad: he promises to come and he doesn't, and he never pays us alimony.

Shame: I was ashamed when the children at school told me they knew my parents were not living together.

Hurt:	I was very hurt when Diana didn't invite me to her birthday party.
Fear:	I'm afraid of Dad. On Sunday he broke our telly and Mum had to call the police.
Jealousy:	I'm jealous of my father's girlfriend's son. My dad bought him a new bike and didn't buy me one.
Anger:	I'm angry with my mum for agreeing to Dad's leaving home.
Longing:	I'm longing for the time when we were all together at home. I wish my parents would return to each other and we'd all live together.
Love:	I love everybody except my father [*breaks into tears*]. I don't think he loves me. He is trying to skimp, so he doesn't come on my birthday.

Ice Breakers

Cards on which the words *If only...* and *If...* are used as stimuli are very effective in encouraging open communication. The use of these cards helps participants express their problems in a playful and non-threatening way.

Helen got the card that said:

> If your radio were to talk about you, what would it say?

She burst out with:

> This is to announce that Helen purposely puts on Michael Jackson's music because Dad's new wife can't stand it. She calls it 'noise'!

We try to illustrate the cards humorously. As previously noted, children should enjoy themselves in the group: this is the time in their life when they need fun and pleasure very badly.

What if your shoes were
to talk about you?
What would they say?

What if your comb were to talk
about you? What would it tell?

If I were to turn into an animal,
I'd choose to be a........................
because..

If I were to be a game,
I'd choose to be............
....
because...........................

If I were a musical instrument,
I'd choose to be a............................
because..

Were I to be food, I'd choose
to be..
because.......................................

If only I could hear....................
....
I'd want that because................

If only my parents..................
....
then...

If only there really were..............
....
then..

If only they'd take me...........
....
then...

If only I could see..........................
....
then I would................................

Sculpture

Clay

Modelling clay is a very useful material for working both with individual youngsters and with groups of children of all ages. Oaklander (1978) believes clay promotes the working through of the most primal of internal processes.

> It affords an opportunity for flow between itself and the user unequalled by any other material. It is easy to become one with the clay. It offers both tactile and kinaesthetic experience. It brings people closer to their feelings. Perhaps because of the flowing quality, a union occurs between the medium and the user. It often seems to penetrate the protective armour, the barriers in a child. (p. 67)

After a short period during which the new group participants play with some clay or plasticine put in front of them, and feel the messy, soft and appealing material in their hands, they are invited to create something that symbolises them. It can be something that they like, something that they are going through in their lives, or something that is part of their world. A child who has finished puts the product on the table, and each member tries to guess what it represents in the 'sculptor's' life. This activity opens new levels of shared thoughts, feelings and experiences, leading to greater intimacy in the group.

Tower

The children in one group were told to build any tower they liked with the clay, as long as it did not exceed the height of the notebook on the table and wouldn't topple over. The children worked seriously and elaborated on the theme, some of them creating a whole new world. When they were ready, we asked them to tell the stories about their 'towers'.

> Simon, aged seven, clothed his 'tower' in toilet paper, making a skirt and a scarf around the 'head'. 'This is the woman who is waiting for her husband' he said. 'She thinks he has gone to the army and she's waiting and waiting for him to come, but no, he isn't there... he went to another woman, he went to *her* children – he doesn't care at all, and she's crying all the time... so the father came home after a long time and when he saw her crying he got angry and started hitting her!

This is the first 'window' we had into Simon's world. A non-verbal child, Simon had at last been able to express himself, verbally, through this medium.

Living Statues

The participants in the group act out various feelings, by turning into 'living statues'. The children are not allowed to use words, only body language. They try to find different ways of expressing anger, fear, sadness, happiness or other feelings. The other participants guess their feelings and then there is a discussion. With younger children, balloons are used: after playing around with the balloons, dancing to music and other games, the children are asked to imagine the balloon is a person who makes them feel happy, angry, and so on – and then to talk about it to the group. Sometimes the group leader helps them act out their feelings and any conflicts arising from these feelings.

Understanding Feelings

Multiple Choice

A picture of a person in a certain mood or situation is introduced. The children are asked to identify the feeling expressed in the picture. There is no 'correct' answer; the leader encourages a variety of reactions while accepting the personal reactions of the children to the stimulus introduced.

Alternatively, the children create captions for the pictures from the following multiple choice possibilities: this helps them to develop a vocabulary for describing their emotions.

	angry		he received a new bike.
	sad		he doesn't have a permit for his new bike and a policeman is standing in the street.
Tom is		because	
	happy		his bike broke down.
	afraid		

	sad		she has to do her homework and she doesn't feel like it.
	afraid		she did her sums correctly.
Sheila is		because	
	glad		the teacher is angry.
	angry		she doesn't understand how to do her arithmetic homework.

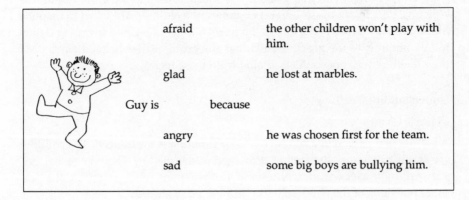

	afraid		the other children won't play with him.
	glad		he lost at marbles.
Guy is		because	
	angry		he was chosen first for the team.
	sad		some big boys are bullying him.

	happy		Grandma is very ill.
	angry		it's her birthday.
Maria is		because	
	sad		her new dress is dirty.
	afraid		she is not allowed to walk around offering her birthday cake to her friends.

Talking Balls

To help shy and reticent children 'open up', we introduce the 'Question-Ball' game. The facilitator begins by posing neutral questions and gradually leads up to more personal ones. As they catch the ball, the children answer promptly. Some sample questions are:

- Who is your favourite teacher?
- Which subject do you hate at school?
- Which is your favourite smell?
- What makes you angry?

This is how the game developed in one group of ten-year-olds.

> In answer to 'What makes you angry?' Jamie answered: 'That my parents got divorced,' and Lily responded: 'That my father doesn't come to visit me.'

As in other activities, here too there is a possibility of removing stigmas, building awareness, empathy and sincerity, and having hear-to-heart talks. The next step in the game is having the children themselves lead the game.

Jamie (as leader in a mixed group) asked:

Which was the happiest day in your life?

Among the answers this question stimulated were:

When I had my birthday.

When my brother was born.

When my parents decided not to divorce.

When my father dies. [*This child's father had deserted the family because of a new relationship.*]

The group-leader reacted with:

> Sometimes someone is so angry that he or she even wants somebody
> dead.

The group then began sharing secret feelings of anger and ways of 'channelling'
them.

The Family Map

This activity consists of a game-board divided into squares, and coloured
figures, representing the various members of the family: mother, father, brother,
sister, grandmother, grandfather, uncle, aunt, mother's boyfriend, father's girlfriend, father's wife, mother's husband, stepbrothers and stepsisters.

The participants are introduced to the board which represents the life space
of the family. The child is invited to place a doll or other object representing her-
or himself in the centre of the board and then to put the figures representing
other family members of the family at appropriate distances, thus expressing
feelings of closeness or distance towards each member of the family. Through
shifting the figures on the board, family relationships can be understood and
worked through.

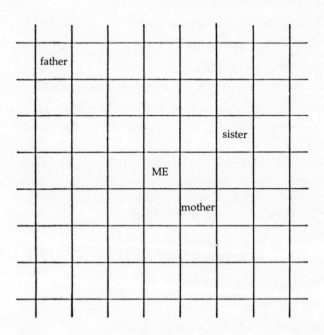

Figure 9.3

When it was Ian's turn to arrange the figures, he put one outside the board, shouting:

> I don't want Dad at all! I don't want to meet him at all and Mum just forces me. She says that he won't give us alimony when we get the divorce if I don't agree to meet him. But I just don't want to meet him. I hate him!

We asked Ian to choose a child from the group who would represent his father. With the help of his friend, he role-played what went on between himself and his father. The second step was to ask the children to exchange roles. Ian's friend was Ian, while Ian himself took his father's role. While acting as Father, Ian said:

> I love my son and I want to spend some time with him!

Thanks to the role-playing, Ian reached a certain degree of insight and understanding of his father's plight and feelings, and found new ways for positive communication between them.

Ruth, on the other hand, put *herself* outside the board. She explained to the children in the group that ever since her mother had brought John to live with them, she feels unwanted in the family. Her mother doesn't tell her anything any more, and neither does she take her into her bed – like she used to. She is only interested in John.

The whole new family was invited for a few sessions and played similar games. Ruth was given the opportunity to express her feelings of being both unwanted and a stranger in the family. A much-needed confrontation between the members of the family occurred, which led to the beginning of a new chapter in their relationships.

Let's Say...

Let's Say... is a good sequel to 'Family Map'. With the help of the following cards, the participants see themselves in the eyes of others. These exercises give them the opportunity of 'stepping into the shoes' of members of their family, as well as those of significant others.

The child chooses a card and 'becomes' the person the card names, speaking in the first person.

Let's say your brother is talking about you. What does he say?

Let's say you are your
neighbour. What do you
tell us about you?

Let's say your friend
is talking about you.
What does he say?

Let's say your grandfather
is telling us about you.
What does he say?

Let's say your step-sister
is telling us about you.
What does she say?

Let's say the friend you've just fought with is telling us about you. What does she say?

Let's say your dog is telling us about you. What does it say?

Let's say your teacher is talking about you. What does she say?

Let's say you are your dad. Please tell us about your child. (About his behaviour, his feeling, etc...)

Let's say you are your grandma.
Please tell us abour your
grandchild.

The Word Basket

We put cards of various colours in a basket. A trigger-word is printed on each card. With their eyes closed, each participant takes one card from the basket, tells a story, and is rewarded with a plastic chip. The words take on a personal meaning for the child: mother, father, son, daughter, hate, love, fight, money, doctor, stupid, bicycle, healthy, angry, kill, accident, present, picture, hospital, and so on. Gardener (1976), who has presented this game in its original version, claims that 'the pressure of unconscious material is more powerful than the contaminating effect of the eliciting stimulus'.

Thelma, aged seven, took out a card with the word 'father' on it. She refused to tell a story. Instead she asked the therapist a question.

> Adina, have you ever killed anybody? [*pause*] I haven't really, but my anger kills.

After a long silence she continued:

> I always make my father mad... and he starts hitting me. Mother interferes and then they begin to fight and Dad wants to leave home. My parents parted once because of me, and now my anger will kill him.

After hearing Thelma's secret fears, the group helped her realise the difference between thoughts and actions.

The Trust Walk

In addition to building trust in the group, the aim of this exercise is to create a metaphoric contract, showing the children the three main areas – feelings, thoughts and behaviours – that will be dealt with in the sessions, and helping them to understand the differences.

The group-leader asks each child to move around the room and stop in front of someone he or she does not feel very close to. One of member of each pair is blindfolded; the other leads. The children are allowed to lead each other over hurdles and under, for example, tables and chairs. After a period of time, the children exchange roles. The one who was on a 'trust walk' now leads his or her partner.

After they have all returned, they share what they thought and felt and how they behaved, both when they were 'blind' and when they led the 'blind'. Their answers are then written on a board, which may begin to look something like this:

	I felt	I thought	I behaved
When 'blind'	afraid	she might make me fall	I peeked
When leading	worried that I'd make a mistake	that this is not so easy to do	I looked ahead very carefully

They then discuss which role they preferred – leading or being led. In future sessions, this chart is often recalled, to helping the children remember the differences between feelings, thoughts and behaviour.

The Balloon Feeling Game

This activity is recommended for the very young (5–9-year-olds).

Children are asked to float around the room, to the sound of music, as if they are balloons of various sizes. Next, they are asked to choose partners: one pretends to be a balloon, which the other blows up; then they exchange roles. Then each is given the chance to choose a *real* balloon and dance around the room with it.

Sitting down, contemplating their own balloons, the children are asked to visualise someone who has angered them greatly:

> *Notice how his or her face looks when you are angry at him or her.*

Maria: I can see Joe, Mum's new husband. I'm so angry with him. Before, even though Mum and Dad were divorced, Dad came to visit me when I was ill, but now Joe won't let him... I didn't see Dad for two whole weeks the last time I was sick.

Ted: I can see my little brother. He's always touching my toys and never lets me do my homework, and then Mum shouts at me.

Hilary: I see my Dad. I'm so angry with him. Why did he leave? What made him travel so far away without telling me? If I'd known I'd have been a good girl. I didn't mean to fight with Dana...

After airing their angry feelings, the children are asked to see in the balloon someone they love very much:

> *Notice what her or his face looks like when you show her or him your love.*

Ted: I can see my little brother. He's so cute. [*This is the very same brother he saw when he was looking for someone to be angry with.*]

Sally: I can see my Grandma. She is the loveliest person in the world. I love her – with her I always feel safe.

Hilary: I see Dad's new baby. I love him. I wish I could go and live with Dad and his new wife. She never shouts at me, and she speaks to me.

Tiktin and Cobb (1983) suggest a variation on the same theme. In their groups they also use balloons to establish a common language for the children and the therapist to use as a basis for communication. Their game begins with the children identifying feelings and listing them on the board. Each child uses a felt marker to draw a face on a balloon, depicting one of the feelings as it relates to the divorce in their families. The children take turns sharing their balloons with the group and describing how they experienced the feeling and how they behaved in connection with it. Different ideas for handling the feelings are exchanged. To conclude the exercise, several balloons (representing feelings) are crowded into a paper bag (representing a person), to demonstrate what happens when too many unexpressed emotions build up inside: a person becomes overloaded. If the feelings are talked about, then the bad feelings do not build up and there is more room for other feelings.

Touching

> A friend of mine travelling in Mexico saw a beautiful child and asked permission of the mother to photograph him. She was pleased by the request, but when the photographer was leaving, she stopped him and said, 'Touch him,' and then she added, 'A child that is not touched will be unlucky.' (Laura Huxley 1963)

One of the highly recommended ways of giving a participant a sense of belonging, a sense of being loved and meaningful to other humans, is working in the group with 'Touch Therapy' or 'Skin Strategies' (Colton 1988). Children of divorced parents may often be rather neglected by parents who, immersed in their own traumatic reactions, have no time or inclination to pet, hug or touch their offspring. If people touched more, there would be much less grief, anxiety and deep feelings of inadequacy (Dunne, Bruggen and O'Brian 1982).

The following are a few strategies introduced by Simon (1974). The exercises have been found to be very successful, enhancing group cohesiveness and tenderness among members.

Massage Train

The group, as usual, sits in a circle. The therapist suggests:

> *Please turn to the right and put your hands on the shoulders of the person there. Bring some comfort to the tired shoulders of the person you are touching. Make your hands healing, comforting, soothing, full of caring.*

At the beginning the children show some apprehension, usually expressed by giggling, tickling or pressing too hard on their neighbours, but the soothing voice of the facilitator, and the fact that he or she also participates, help the children settle down. After a while,

Figure 9.3

> *Slowly, let your hands come to a rest but don't take them away yet. Cradle your friend's shoulders in your caring hands. And then, slowly, take your hands away.*

After a short pause, the next instruction is:

> *Now turn around and put your hands on the shoulders of the person who massaged you.*

Temple Caring

The group is divided into pairs. They pick their own partners, compare heights, and then form two sub-groups: 'shorties' and 'longies'. However, anyone who has always been a 'shortie' and wants to be a 'longie' can choose to be one, and *vice versa*. One group is then asked to sit on chairs.

> *Keep your eyes closed until I tell you to open them. Longies, stand behind a shortie and touch him or her gently on the top of the head. Shortie, keep your eyes closed. Later on you'll find out who your secret partner is. Longie, lean your shortie's head gently against your body and begin to stroke her or his temples in the most gentle caring way you can.*

After about three minutes the facilitator says:

> *Let your hands gradually come to a rest and cradle your partner's head ever so lightly between your hands. Let your partner feel safe there, with the warmth and tenderness and healing quality of your loving hands. Slowly take your hands away and come around the front and let your shorties see who was there for them.*

After a second round the partners change places and the exercise begins again. Later on, the group shares what each one has experienced. The children have developed self-awareness, as well as having become calm, soothed and more aware of the other members of the group.

Head and Body Tapping

This activity again takes place in pairs. The facilitator says:

> *Stand behind your partner, curve your fingers and tap gently on the person's head, like raindrops falling. Check with the person receiving the raindrops to learn if they are too hard or too soft – no-one should suffer any discomfort. Everyone: try to get into the same rhythm, tapping gently to the same beat. Then, suddenly take your hands away – now!*

Everyone feels a sudden release, often causing laughter – the 'tappees' because their scalps tingle and the 'tappers' because their fingertips feel so alive.

Talking Hands

The children pair off again. The leader asks them to hold each others' hands, to shut their eyes, and to let their hands 'do the talking'. Sometimes the children show each other love with their hands, sometimes they are mischievous, sometimes angry, sometimes the hands simply relax together. After a while the children are asked to open their eyes and share their experiences with the group.

Chinese Puzzle

This exercise was introduced by Morris and Cinnamon (1975). It has proved to be a very good exercise for exploring members' feelings about close physical contact, bringing them closer to each other and building trust. It is very popular with the children.

The facilitator asks the group for a volunteer who is willing to solve a puzzle. The volunteer is then asked to leave the room, and the rest of the members stand up, form a circle, and join hands.

They then intertwine themselves as completely as possible without breaking contact (for example, going under, around, above each other, so that they become a mass of closely knit bodies. The volunteer is then brought back into the room and is told to verbally, not physically, instruct members to untangle without breaking contact at any time. After the circle is re-formed, the group members discuss the experience.

Usually the children beg to go on and on; each wants a turn at untangling. Often, during discussions in the group, this exercise has led the conversation, metaphorically, to the entanglement of their lives, as well as being very useful for the enhancement of group cohesiveness.

CHAPTER TEN

Group Sessions

Once the group has been 'launched', and the children have learned to work together comfortably, the following activities are very productive.

E.T. From Outer Space

We have adopted a strategy introduced by Simon and O'Rourke (1977) in *Developing Values with Exceptional Children,* for working with very young children of divorced parents. The strategy helps the children both to pinpoint the difficulties of their present circumstances and to recognise the positive aspects of their lives.

The children are seated in a semi-circle in front of a board covered with drawing paper; a tray in front of the board offers an inviting collection of water-colours and paint-brushes. The therapist tells a story, using lots of mime and dramatisations. The story describes a space-craft from an unknown planet that has landed in the schoolyard. (While speaking, the therapist draws a sort of flying saucer on the board in front of the group.) As the door of the space ship opens, there stands one lonely figure who is a child of their own age. The children are asked to use their imaginations and contribute all their ideas to produce a collective drawing of this person on the large piece of paper. After finishing the drawing, the children are asked to name the child. Names like 'Charlie' and 'Susie' have been suggested, but most groups come up with 'E.T.'

The leader then takes down the picture and puts it on the portable board, standing behind it and pretending to be E.T. The children always answer E.T.'s questions very readily. They are called upon to answer two main questions: 'What do you enjoy most about the world you live in?' and 'What do you suffer from most in the world?'

> Clare, an adopted six-year-old girl, told how she hated to be kicked, hit and punished violently by her father during his fights with her mother. She added that she enjoyed visiting her grandparents most, because they never beat her up. She wanted to go and live with them when her parents finally divorced. We investigated the matter and found that Clare was abused. The authorities were called in, and she was put into the care of

her grandparents, her permanent living arrangements to be determined by the court.

Usually the answers are not so dramatic, but the game gives the children the opportunity to express their feelings and thoughts about the upheaval of their present lives.

Balance Sheet

An activity that enhances group interaction and helps children feel they are sharing a common goal is writing out, together, lists of things that are 'different' and things that are 'the same' after their parents' divorce. Tiktin and Cobb (1983) believe that the lists show the children that many families undergo similar changes after divorce, that some things do not change and that improvements (such as less fighting at home) can occur.

> Shirley's parents had told her that they were planning to divorce and that she would be living with her father. The eleven-year-old was devastated, feeling that her world was crumbling. She was so depressed that the school counsellor decided to let her join a group of children of divorce who had begun working together a few months earlier. The leader asked the children to help Shirley by making a list of things that are 'different' and 'the same' before and after the divorce.

The following are a few of the things the children dictated.

DIFFERENT

(*Robert*) There are children who tell me that now I concentrate more in my studies. It's true, because when we lived in the same house, they were always fighting, and I used to think about it at school. Now I feel so free.

(*Nina*) The divorce made my grades go down.

(*Nina*) I see my father much more now than I used to when my parents were together.

(*Maria*) You are only half a family. There are many contracts, but half the family lost

(*Robert*) Before the divorce, my parents treated me very badly. I

SAME

(*Hilary*) I've remained just the same as I used to be before the divorce; I've always had good grades at school.

(*Peter*) Socially, I feel exactly the same with my friends. Nothing's changed.

(*Guy*) I'm studying again as well as I used to before. It was only for a short time that my schoolwork was no good.

(*Alistair*) I have the same problem with friends that I used to have. When I lived together with Mum and Dad, I missed many meetings with my friends because I had to stay home in case they fought. Today, I also miss meetings, because I used to run away because there were fights at home. After the divorce, Dad started treating me much better. He tried to console me. have to spend time with each parent separately. I just don't have enough time, so I miss out on trips and fun with my friends.

At this stage, Shirley joined in, asking to list her remarks in the 'different' column.

In my family, it is exactly like in Robert's. My Dad is very tense. He goes out early and comes back very late. Mum is very nervous and angry. This worries me very much, because when I live with my Dad only, I will be alone a lot. I want to be with both of them.

Learning About Patterns of Response

Despite similarities in their response patterns, children are convinced that they are unique in their thoughts, feelings and reactions and are inclined to blame themselves and others without considering or testing reality. They may be ashamed of their circumstances and incapable of dealing with their everyday world. The following card game can be used both to help them learn about possible response patterns and to guide their choices of suitable responses. The game has the added benefit of encouraging the non-verbal child to speak. Ten common response patterns are highlighted.

Adam, aged nine, suffered quite badly from his parents' divorce. He found it impossible to pay attention at school, his studies deteriorated alarmingly and he 'closed up'. He did not cooperate with adults and refused to participate in a group for children of divorce. After some persuasion, he agreed to sit in the counsellor's room, at her side, but without any verbal response. One day the counsellor lay the cards of the 'Divorce Card Game' in front of him. Suddenly he was heard murmuring: 'You know, it wasn't at all like this for me... I wasn't ashamed... I just closed my brain and pretended I wasn't me!'

This incident immediately opened up avenues of communication between the child and the counsellor.

The game is played as follows:

Preparation: Prepare four matching cards for each response-pattern category. Every card has a title (the response-pattern category) and presents four options. Although the text of the four cards in every set is identical, each card emphasises a different statement. (For example, on one card, Option A is underlined or printed in a different colour; on a matching card, Option B is emphasised, etc.). (This game is very similar to the 'Happy Families' game.)

Playing the   After the cards are shuffled, the participants each receive four
game: cards at random, and try to create a 'foursome' by asking for
                 the cards they lack. After all the series have been collected,
                 and are lying on the table, the participants discuss the
                 various meanings of the response patterns and their
                 usefulness for normal adjustment.

'Event cards': An 'Event card' sets a scene, such as the following:

Every now and then David remembers **that evening** – the one when his
parents tell him about their decision to divorce. At first he can't believe his
ears. He looks at his parents and notices their expressions. Only then does
he realise that they are serious. What happens to David?

Response-Pattern Cards

IF ONLY...

a. If only I had been a good boy, this wouldn't have happened.

b. If only they had told me beforehand about the situation, I could have convinced
them.

c. If only Mum and Dad were to ask someone who understood and could help,
they would make up!

d. If only they would give in to each other, we could just go on being together.

WHAT SHOULD I DO?

a. Maybe I should discuss it with John; his parents also got divorced a year ago.

b. The counsellor seems to know about such problems; maybe he'll be able to
help me?

c. I'll go to the library and read books about divorce.

d. I'll find out from my parents who I'm going to live with.

WHO'S MISERABLE?

a. All this divorce business has hurt me terribly.

b. I'm sad most of the time and feel I want to cry.

c. I'm afraid that when one of my parents remarries, she or he won't pay attention
to me any more.

d. I often ask myself: 'What'll happen to me?'

AS LONG AS NOBODY FINDS OUT!

a. I'll tell them my Dad's away on business, or abroad.

b. I won't invite friends home.

c. I'll talk about trips and good times I've had with both parents.

d. I'll make Mum and Dad come to school events together.

EXCUSES

a. My parents have the right to decide about their own lives.

b. At long last it will be quiet at home, after all the fighting.

c. Now I won't have to justify every single movement I make.

d. I know they are getting divorced, but they're still going to go on being my parents.

WHO'S TO BLAME?

a. Dad's to blame – he's always angry and shouting at home.

b. Mum's to blame – she's always getting mad about something.

c. It's all because of Grandma and Grandpa; they're forever interfering in what goes on in our home.

d. I made my parents angry many times and they fought because of me.

I HAVE NO LUCK!

a. Everything always happens to me.

b. I suppose that's the way it had to happen.

c. There's nothing I can do to change the situation.

d. Our family has no luck.

IT CAN'T BE TRUE!

a. It can't be true – it seems like a bad dream.

b. It's impossible that such things should happen to me.

c. They're just saying it; in the end, I'm sure they'll make up and stay together.

d. To me, it doesn't matter if they're together or not.

WHAT'S IN IT FOR ME?

a. The teacher will consider what I'm going through and will exempt me from many assignments.

b. The children will give in and let me win lots of games.

c. Everyone will try to help me.

d. Now both Mum and Dad will spoil me and buy me lots of presents.

I SHALL OVERCOME!

a. I'm strong enough to cope with the new situation.

b. My achievements at school have returned to what they were before.

c. I don't think so much about the divorce any more.

d. I'm not so ashamed any more to reveal that my parents are divorced.

Bingo

The purpose of this game is to deepen the group's mutual acquaintance, allowing the members to work with metaphors if they prefer to do so. It has also been shown to encourage children's self-disclosure during discussions.

The children are given paper and pencil to write down their names, and then to write any piece of information about themselves which they feel makes them unique from the other members. They can also write or draw something that symbolises them, if they wish. They then hand in the folded pages to the therapist.

Each child then receives a large sheet of paper, and folds it so that the creases create as many squares as there are group members. The child then fills in the name of one participant in each square.

The facilitator says:

> I will now read out what the members have written about themselves, without telling you who wrote what. Try to figure out who wrote the note I am reading, and jot it's contents down in the box with that person's name.

The results resemble the table below:

Susan	Miriam	Robert	David	Anna
a flower [Susan had drawn a flower]	hates exams	loves football	is always angry	loves watching telly
Rachel	**Michael**	**Dan**	**Sarah**	
loves coming to group sessions	loves his computer	wishes his parents would get together again	loves her stepfather	

This game leads to interesting discussions about how the children see each other.

The 'Symbol' Guessing Game

The children are asked to write down all the names of the members in the group, including their own. They are then asked to write down something that symbolises each one in the group, including themselves.

Each member then listens to what has been said about him or her, without saying what they have written about themselves. Each member must explain why she or he has chosen specific symbols.

Sarah to Michael: I chose a snail for you, because in the beginning you always hid inside your shell, but now you've begun to peep out.

Miriam to Robert: I chose a football for you, because you're forever kicking a football.

Birthdays

One of the most important activities in groups for children of divorce is the celebration of birthdays. At the very beginning, everyone's birthday is marked on a calendar, and when the day comes, special attention is given to the child. Everyone in the group talks about the celebrant's good points, making sure to mention what he or she has already managed to cope with and has achieved with the group. We give each birthday-child imaginary presents, something that suits his or her character, and at the end, a few real birthday gifts as well. The child is also asked to talk about his or her feelings in the group.

These celebrations contribute greatly to the child's self-esteem and happiness, and makes the child feel loved by the members in the group.

Figure 10.1

CHAPTER ELEVEN

Further Group Sessions
Values Clarification

Introducing Values Clarification

A crisis in the family creates such confusion that previously learned patterns of behaviour often cannot assist adjustment to the changed conditions. A new sort of 'compass' is needed for finding one's way in the unknown territory of divorce.

The parents who are in the midst of a crisis are not emotionally available for their children and are unable to suggest or find solutions for the child who is entangled in confusion and embarrassment. It is important to encourage these children to develop the ability to reexamine their situations and find ways to lessen and clarify the vagueness and the uncertainty. 'Values Clarification' (VC) is particularly suitable for this purpose. This system helps children deal with conflict-fraught situations that require deliberation, choice, and decision-making. Its aim is to give individuals the ability to appraise their own behaviour consciously and choose suitable means of behaviour for themselves. It clarifies unclear issues and helps develop positive ways of coping, such as adaptability, confidence in the face of challenges, initiative, creativity and decisiveness (Shectman 1980).

VC was developed as an educational method and has been found to be most efficient in treating children from families undergoing divorce. Based on principles that direct the individual towards specific future goals and offer alternative approaches towards those goals, it has been used not only in parent counselling, but also to treat children in groups and individually.

Although the original purpose of this method was to activate intrapsychic processes in the individual, its use as a group system has been found to be more effective in developing motivation and courage. The group enables the giving and receiving of feedback and support and develops tolerance and flexibility towards varied attitudes and reactions.

The aims of the process are (Howe and Howe 1975):

1. To resist external pressures when having to choose how to react.

2. To be able to choose from a number of solutions to a given problem.

3. To weigh responsibly the consequences or results of each alternative solution.

4. To evaluate each alternative independently, according to possible results.

5. To share the process of choice with others and to openly espouse the values chosen.

6. To act consistently and with perseverance according to those values.

Through the process of choosing preferred aims and reactions, the child learns to see him- or herself clearly and to recognise the connection between hidden expectations, declared aims and possible modes of action. This awareness leads to identification of those expectations, which can then be fulfilled.

The participants are invited to assess the connections between their deeds and their consequences without any pressure of judgement or criticism. They are given the opportunity to reevaluate the incidents in their lives over which they have no control or influence (such as war, financial losses, death, divorce or a parent's illness), to learn how to come to terms with events that cannot be changed, and to recognise where meaningful exchanges can be made, such as in their emotional reactions to events. They are encouraged to search actively for support in the actions that will fulfil their needs.

The Values Clarification method suggests ways to promote cognitive processes, facilitate the expression of feelings and encourage performance. These experiences influence personal independence and enhance responsibility and social cooperation (Gottlieb and Shimron 1982). The process involves asking leading and clarifying questions (Simon, Howe and Kirschenbaum 1978).

Clarifying Questions

- How long have you felt this way?

- How have you reached this conclusion?

- What influenced you?

These questions do not have one clearly defined answer or solution, but leave the final decision to the participant.

The Clarifying Interview

The clarifying interview focuses on the individual in order to help her or him identify values, examine feelings about them and move toward their actualisation. Issues that might be explored are:

- Principles and attitudes of which interviewees are proud
- Things that disturb interviewees in their social milieux

- Things interviewees are prepared to fight for.

Clarification Strategies

Clarification strategies are based on exercises that help the group identify the values which are important to each individual, examine their meanings, and share them with the others. For example:

- *The strategy of personal preferences:* classifying and ranking actions according to personal preferences, explaining them while doing so
- *Ranking on a continuum:* finding each individual's location on continua between polarities of characteristics or behaviours.

The next two pages present written forms which help children evaluate their own behaviour on continua.

Evaluating and Ranking Behaviour

Mum and Dad are fighting and shouting. Some children react to this by crying.

What happens to YOU? Mark the place on the line that best describes your reaction.

	1	2	3	4	5	6	7	8	9	10	
I never cry	_	_	_	_	_	_	_	_	_	_	*I always cry*

Are you pleased with the place where you have put yourself?.....................................
....
Why did you choose this place? ....
....
Would you like to change this place? ....
If so, to which number?...
How would you do that?...

When parents fight with each other, often they also shout at their children. Children who become angry sometimes start kicking and hitting their brothers and sisters.

How do YOU behave? Mark the place on the line that best describes your behaviour.

| | 1 | 2 | 3 | 4 | 5 | 6 | 7 | 8 | 9 | 10 | |

*I never hit
or kick my
brothers
and sisters*
           *I always hit
and kick my
brothers and
sisters*

Why did you choose this place? ....

....

Give an example..

....

Are you pleased with this place?..

Would you like to change this behaviour? ....

Which place would you like to reach? ....

What could you do to reach that place?..

....

There are some children who are afraid of losing their parents when they are about to divorce, so they start clinging to them.

How do YOU behave? Mark the place on the line that best describes your behaviour.

| | 1 | 2 | 3 | 4 | 5 | 6 | 7 | 8 | 9 | 10 | |

*I cut myself
off comp-
letely from
my parents.*
           *I always
cling to
my parents*

Why did you choose this place? ....

....

Give an example..

....

Would you like to behave differently? ....

Which place would you like to reach? ....

What could you do to reach that place?..

....

Who could help you? ....

Using Multiple Choice Questions to Identify Reactions

Children feel different things when their parents fight with each other or decide to divorce, and they often find it difficult to decide how to behave. The following questions, discussed with the group, help them assess their behaviour.

Here are a few things that children feel. Underline what best describes how YOU feel.

- I'm confused.
- I don't want to play with my friends.
- I don't feel like doing anything.
- I don't believe adults anymore.

Questions for clarification

- Are you pleased with your feeling?
- If not, how would you change it?
- Who could help you?
- How would you act?

When my parents talk of divorce

- I cry all the time.
- I feel guilty.
- I am scared that they don't love me.
- I'm really anxious – what's going to happen?

Questions for clarification

- Are you pleased with your feeling?
- If not, how would you change it?
- Who could help you?
- How would you act?

When my parents fight each other terribly

- I hide my head under the pillow so that I won't hear them.
- I feel as though I were falling into a deep bottomless pit, and I don't know what to do.
- I try to get them to make up.
- I begin crying as if something hurts me, so that they'll forget about the fight and come to me instead.

Questions for clarification

- Are you pleased with your feeling?
- If not, how would you change it?
- Who could help you?
- How would you act?

When Mum and Dad shout at each other

- It's difficult for me to decide who is right.
- I run away.
- I understand that they're both right and wrong.

Questions for clarification

- Are you pleased with your feeling?
- If not, how would you change it?
- Who could help you?
- How would you act?

Denial

In the first stages of therapy, denial reactions are often evident. Sometimes the child ignores the painful family situations:

> My parents don't fight.

> This doesn't happen to me.

Or, the child denies what these events mean to him or her:

> I don't care!

When one is unaware of one's trials and experiences, including accompanying negative feelings, or when one tries to deny them, there is a danger that these feelings will arise, overflow, and overcome one's powers of deliberation. In this state, a person has no control over emotions. Expressing feelings does not automatically lead to better coping, but examining feelings and perceptions creates a rational and conscious foundation for decisions and actions. When people are aware of feelings such as jealousy, envy, aggression and anxiety, there is a good chance that their decisions will be less distorted.

The following activities are open-ended. The participants are presented with trigger words that are supposed to bring out their vehement feelings.

Sentence Completion

Sentence completion is a projective activity used as a warm-up before engaging in the more complicated activities presented afterwards.

1. Lately I...

2. My Mum and Dad...

3. My Mother...

4. My Dad...

5. The children in my class...

6. I think that...

7. My Grandpa and Grandma...

Anger

After the surrender of denial, anger comes to the fore.

Children must become aware that being angry doesn't mean that a person is evil. It is possible to be angry with parents or brothers and sisters even though one loves them. Some children feel bad about themselves every time they get angry, and some are afraid to talk about it. Other children are so scared of anger that they don't even dare to think about it.

Clarifying Responses to Anger

The following cards help children understand and deal with their own rage. In each card the child is confronted with an annoying situation that provokes her or his anger. The child practices new ways of communication by using Values Clarification techniques. The anger is channelled into healthy self-expression.

Ruth was angry with her father who used to arrive late when they met. She thought that being angry with father was terrible. Her father continued arriving late and Ruth got more and more angry – she felt very bad about herself.

How can Ruth change her feeling?

What should she do?

What do you think will happen?

David is very angry! His parents are divorced, but he wants them to remarry each other. His parents have explained to him that they got divorced because they don't love each other any more and they were very unhappy together, and that they won't remarry each other.

Do you, too, get angry like David?

How do you deal with this anger?

How could you change your feeling?

Kirsten would burst into furious tantrums because her father didn't come to visit her as he had promised. When she realized that her shouting didn't help, she stopped and began to play with other girls, which helped her to overcome her longing. When Kirsten's father did finally arrive, she was calm.

What do you feel when your father doesn't come to visit you the way he promised he would?

Are you able to cope with this feeling?

How could you change this feeling?

What could help you?

How would you act? What will you do?

Maria was very angry because her mother dated another man. After her mother discussed it with her, she realized that her mother had the right to spend time and enjoy herself anyway she wanted. Maria learnt that if she changed her way of thinking about something, it helped her, and she was less angry.

Do you feel like Maria sometimes?

How could you change your feeling?

What will you do?

When we try to get something and don't succeed, and nothing that is suggested (to us) satisfies us, we are angry. We want to get the thing that we wanted in the beginning. Sometimes, however, we decide to give up, and to be satisfied with something else that will be just as good as the thing we want. This is called a substitute.

Have you ever found a substitute instead of getting angry?

How did you do it?

If not, try to find a substitute for your anger now.

Role-Playing

Situations presented for role-playing are worth repeating several times, so that participants can try out and exchange roles.

The parents want David to stay for the Sunday family dinner. David wants to go out with his friends. What happens?

The teacher is collecting money for the annual class trip. Sam has a problem: there isn't enough money at home. What does he say?

Mother asks you to go to the shops. You are in the middle of reading a fascinating story. What do you do?

All the girls are skipping but Diana is standing alone watching them.
What must she do?
How could you help her?

All the children are playing together. Suddenly Samantha's father comes and starts shouting at her, in front of everybody.
What happens?
How do the children react?

Ruth has no good friends. She is sitting at home all alone and very sad. Some children from her class come over and try to talk her into going out with them. What is she going to do?

Dana's mother came to school and told the teacher that she and her husband were getting divorced. A few of the children heard her. What happened?

You are trying to fall asleep and your parents start fighting. What do you do?

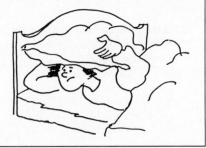

Mother said to Father:
'Your children and my children are beating up our children!'
What happens?
How is this problem solved?

What do you love about your
mother?
How do you show it to her?

How does your elder brother/ sister
help you?
What do you feel when your
brother/sister helps you?
What could you do so that your
brother/sister would help you
more?

How do you help your father?
What do you feel when you help
your father? Are there things with
which you would like to help him
more? What could you do?

What does your father do best?
Are you pleased with this?
What would you
like him to do best?

How does Grandma help you?
What do you feel when Grandma
helps you?
What could you do so that
Grandma will help you more?

How does your Grandpa help you?
What do you feel when your
Grandpa helps you?
What could you do so that Grandpa
will help you more?

How does your Mum help you?
What do you feel when your
mother helps you?
What could you do to make your
mother help you more?

Sometimes children lie to their
parents because they know that
telling the truth will get them into
trouble more that lying. Have you
ever lied to your father? What
happened? How did you feel when
you lied? Could you have acted
otherwise?

How does your father help you?
What do you feel when your father
helps you?
What could you do so that your
father will want to help you?

What do you love about your father?
How do you show it to him?

What is the most exciting
experience that has ever happened
to you with your parents?
What could you do to have it
happen again? Who could help you?

Members of a family have both
duties and rights. Do your parents
have more rights than you do? If so,
what are the rights? Would you like
to have more rights at home? How
could you achieve more rights for
yourself at home?

How do you help your mother?
What do you feel when you help
your mother?
Are there any more things you
would like to help her with?
What could you do?

What does your father believe in
most?
What does your mother believe in
most?
What do you believe in most?
What do you find in common
between your beliefs and your
parents' beliefs?

What does your mother do best?
Are you pleased with this?
What would you like her to do best?

What do your parents love about
you?
Why do they love just this about
you?
What other things would you want
them to love about you?
What must you do?

How do you feel when you are with
your parents?
Why do you feel like that?
Would you like to feel different?
What should you do to change your
feelings?

Have you ever fought with your
parents?
Why was it about?
Did you make up?
Were you pleased with the way you
behaved?

Remarriage of Either or Both Parents

The following activities are introduced to help the child adjust to the remarriage of parents. As before, sentence-completion activities serve as a warm-up before beginning role-playing.

Before Rachel's mother had met her stepfather, Rachel and her mother used to spend a lot of time together talking and having a good time. They were together every evening. After Rachel's mother married again, her new husband brought his little three-year-old daughter, Susan, to live with them. Now, the days of having fun together are over. Rachel's mother is busy all day, and Rachel feels that she spends more time with Susan than with her.

Complete and answer

Rachel feels...towards her new father.
Rachel feels...towards her mother.
Rachel feels...towards Susan.

Can you suggest to Rachel a few ways of changing her feelings towards these people? What should she do?

Harry was used to spending every Saturday morning with his father, but ever since his father met his new wife, their habits have changed. Now, every Saturday morning the family goes to visit the step-grandmother.

Complete and answer

How do you think Harry feels? ....

....

What makes him feel that way? ....

....

Has anything similar ever happened to you? ....

....

What did you do? ....

....

How did you feel? ....

....

Could you have acted differently? ....

....

Who could have helped you? ....

....

Andrew's mother came to the parent–teacher meeting with her new husband. Andrew was ashamed.

Judy's mother also arrived at school with her new husband, but Judy was very glad.

Complete and answer

Has something similar ever happened to you? ....

....

How did you feel? ....

....

Would you have liked to change your feelings? ....

....

How? ....

....

On Saturday Graham visited his Dad's new family. He was playing with Sharon, his father's new wife's little daughter, when she suddenly burst out crying very loudly. Graham didn't understand what had happened.

His father's wife came into the room and shouted and blamed Graham. Graham tried again and again to explain what had happened, but she didn't seem at all interested in his explanation. He felt very hurt.

Complete and answer

What did Graham feel? ....

What did he do? ....

....

Has something similar ever happened to you? ....

....

Were you pleased with the way you acted? ....

....

Could you have acted differently? ....

....

What could you have done? ....

....

Hannah's teacher told the counsellor that ever since her parents' decision to divorce, Hannah sits and daydreams in class.

- Does this happen to you too?
- Do you mind this?
- If so, how can you change it?

There are some children who stop eating when there are problems between their parents.

- What do they want to achieve by acting in this way?
- What do they gain this way?
- What do they lose?
- How can one manage without eating?
- Has something like this ever happened to you?
- How could you change it?

There are some children who don't want to play with their friends when their parents fight or get divorced.

- Have you also experienced something like this?
- Why did this happen to you?
- How do you feel about it?
- Would you like to have changed your behaviour?

Sometimes children whose parents are about to divorce have terrifying nightmares.

- Does it happen to you too?
- If it does, please tell us about your dreams.
- What can you do so that this won't happen again?
- Who could help you?

CHAPTER TWELVE

Closure

Summing Up

The various closure techniques suggested in this chapter are variations on a single theme. They all aim to end the group sessions in a responsible way, bearing in mind the feelings of desertion and loss that children of divorced parents have undergone and making sure that the closure of the group does not become, for them, an additional abandonment trauma.

Towards the end of the group sessions we ask the children to recall other partings and endings that they have experienced – leaving pre-school and kindergarten, parting from parents on the first day of school, parting for the summer holiday, partings from grandparents living far away and, of course, divorce-related partings from parents. The feelings connected with these are ventilated and discussed, and the counsellor starts reminding the group that soon it will be time for the group to end as well.

The last meeting is usually a particularly emotional one. The group members have by now learned to love and be a part of one another's lives, having 'lived through' each other's crises and witnessed their courage and recoveries.

Activities Which Facilitate Closure

Hearts

The children are each given a large heart made of thick paper and a pin, and are asked to pin the heart on the back of another child in the group. They are then given felt-tip pens and told to write on each heart something good they have learned about the member wearing it. It is beautiful to see the children, sometimes standing in a line like a train, each writing on the others' backs.

When they have all written on all of the hearts, they take them off and read them silently. Each participant then reads out what is written on the heart of the child to his or her left. Thus, all the youngsters have the pleasure of hearing, out loud and in public, good things written about them.

Accordion

This is a variation of 'Hearts', only here the children take a large sheet of paper, fold it into an accordion, write their names at the top and pass it round the group. Each child then writes something appropriate to the child whose name is at the top and folds back the paper to cover what has been written. The children are encouraged to write about good things they have learned about each other. Again, when all the children have written on all the sheets of paper, each 'accordion' is read aloud and discussed.

What Am I Taking With Me?

The group, eyes closed, stands in a circle holding hands. The object is to reflect individually on everything that has happened during the sessions and for each child to choose one particular thing that they have learned and which they feel is important and worth taking away for further consideration. The children then open their eyes and tell the others what they have chosen (adapted from Jennings 1986):

> 'What I am taking with me is that I have some friends and am not the only one with problems of divorce,' said Odette. 'I got this at the very first meeting; suddenly I saw children I had seen at school and had had no idea they had the same problem, and here they were in the same group as me. I immediately saw that I wasn't a special kind of zombie, that it happened to others as well!'

Symbolic Feedback

Small cards and felt-tip pens are required for this activity.

The group sits in a circle. Each child is asked to look at the person sitting to the right, and to imagine what gift he or she would like to give that person 'to help her or him on an individual journey, without the group'. This gift could be a specific object, such as a flower or a puppy, or it may perhaps be a quality, such as tenacity. The gifts should be written and drawn, if possible, on the cards, and handed to the neighbouring child. The exercise is then repeated, this time with the child on the left. Discussion follows (Jennings 1986).

'You Gave the Group and Me...'

This strategy has proved very successful with groups of children of divorce. Adapted from *A Handbook of Verbal Group Exercises* (Morris and Cinnamon 1983), the aims of the exercise are to give and receive final feedback before the closure of the group, to consolidate participants' feelings of self-worth, to end the group on a positive note and to achieve, if possible, a highly positive experience.

The facilitator tells the group they will engage in a closure exercise in which they will have the opportunity to thank each other for contributions made to the group and to each other.

Stand in a circle, with arms around each other's waists. One by one, each of you will step into the centre, facing any individual you choose. That person will give you feedback. Then, you will go to another friend to hear feedback. Keep doing this until you have heard from each of the members.

If you are part of the circle, and it's your turn to give feedback to the person in the centre, please say:

'You gave the group..., and you gave me...'

Each member takes his turn in the centre until every member has received feedback from every other member.

The therapist can also suggest alternate phrasings, to provide variety and prevent boredom or loss of motivation.

If it's your turn to give feedback, there are other sentences besides 'You gave the group...' that you can use. Here are some you might prefer:

'If I could take a personal quality of yours and make it mine, I'd take...'

'I love you because...'

'When I first met you, I thought... and now I know...'

The Farewell Party

A final party or get-together, with cake, ice-cream and songs, can be organised to put the closure on a more 'neutral', less emotional footing.

Figure 12.1

CHAPTER THIRTEEN

Vignettes From Group Sessions

The following vignettes allow us a few glimpses into the group sessions of children of divorced parents. We have chosen highlights from a group consisting of boys and girls aged eleven to twelve. Every year, in the school where these sessions took place, we simultaneously conduct three or four groups of children going through the crisis of divorce. The group described in the present chapter met every Tuesday at what we call 'zero hour' – 7.25 a.m., before the day's first lesson. This less-than-serendipitous timing was due to the force of circumstances, as it was important that the children not miss lessons. However, the hours after school are a better choice, as sessions can then continue a little longer, if necessary.

The Second Session

During this session, we engaged in the 'Legend of My Name and Birth' activity. (*Note:* We have changed the real names of the participants and have left out the stories of their names.)

Roy: Mine was a difficult birth. My father had a long list of all the names of family and friends to tell the good news to. I was born on December 25th and I think this is a very unlucky date. My mother told me that the Christians' Jesus was born on this day. I've heard that he was crucified – maybe that's why I've also had such bad luck – my family all broken up. It's an unlucky day to be born on.

Myra: The day I was born I expected my life to be so different. I didn't think my mother would divorce Dad because he became completely paralysed in the army. I didn't know I'd have to live without my brother and sister at Grandma's and Grandpa's. I didn't even want to be born a girl...

Rachel: When I was born my parents couldn't ever agree about my name. Dad wanted me to be Katy and Mum wanted me to be called Rachel, so they each called me something else... from the beginning there was something in the air. At school I'm called Rachel, so please call me Katy in the group.

The Third Session

To create the rules of the group, we each took turns suggesting one rule. The leader began by reminding the children that they could talk about their feelings and thoughts, but were not allowed to tell their parents' secrets unless they had been allowed to do so.

The children volunteered some very meaningful rules:

Myra: We should respect and honour the members, and accept views different from our own. We should 'build' each other, support and help one another.

Judy: We should keep each other's secrets.
[*Here the leader asked all the children to join hands in a circle and take a vow of secrecy. The children felt very excited and much closer to each other after the 'swearing in'.*]

Peter: The most important rule is to speak freely and to trust the group.

Leader: I suggest we should be like mirrors for each other. [*Brings a large mirror and puts it on the table.*] Gather around – let's all look into the mirror together. Do you notice how we see ourselves and we also see each other? The mirror tells me that I have a smudge on my forehead – it doesn't say if it's good or not – just that I have a smudge. I'll decide what to do about it, and whether it's good or not. That's how we'll be in our group – mirrors to each other! We won't judge each other, only give feedback on how things look.

The Fourth Session

One of the girls brought in a decorated poster with all fifteen of our rules neatly written on it. To reinforce and help the children internalise the rules, the counsellor asked each child to read aloud the rule he or she liked best, and explain why.

(The following activity was suggested by Mel Hoffstead.) The leader brought a big poster showing the outline of a child (named 'Molly'), and white stickers which were handed out to all the participants, and said:

What could hurt a child whose parents are getting divorced? On each sticker, write down something that hurts or wrongs a child, that makes him or her suffer. After that we'll stick it onto the figure, on the part of the body that you think hurts the most.

Edna	wrote *longing* and *sadness* on different stickers and stuck them on Molly's head.
Roy	wrote *hurting*, because he'd gone down in his studies, and stuck it on the head too.
Tom	wrote *hurting socially* and explained: 'You miss the fun because you have to spend time both at Dad's and at Mum's. It takes up so much time that you don't have time to be with your friends. You don't know what to do. I'd like to stick this all over the doll's body.'
Paul	wrote *sadness*, *longing*, and *shame*, explaining: 'When Mum invites a boyfriend to our home. I'll stick them all on the heart, because that's where it hurts.'
Jill	wrote *pain* and explained: 'Because of what Dad's done to us.' The children asked her to explain and she told of how her father had left home and moved in with her mother's best friend. (She stuck the sticker on Molly's chest.)

The leader then gave out coloured envelopes and asked the children to write on each one what could help children overcome these hurts. The 'pain' stickers were then put into the envelopes, and the 'help and coping' images now cover the figure, empowering all participants.

A Later Session

During this session, a new girl, Shirley, joined the group. Her parents were just about to divorce and she had been told that she was going to live with her father. Shirley was in the first stage of 'mourning' over the divorce – showing signs of ambiguity and imbalance, seeming very confused, anxious and tearful – and the counsellor decided to enable her to express her feelings and to allow the others in the group to help her.

Shirley:	I'm sorry I was born. I'm sure it's because of me that my parents have always been quarrelling. For instance, last Independence Day we were told to wear white shirts and I took one of Dad's from the closet. When he found out, he beat me up and they fought for days. Now they're getting divorced, and if I hadn't been born they'd still be together – they'd never fight. [*Here the counsellor made a mental note to work on the subject of guilt in the very near future.*]

Ruth:	Don't think that this doesn't happen everywhere. I used to cry when my parents fought and shouted, because I was afraid my father would go away. He always promised that he would never leave me and said that he loved me very much, that I shouldn't worry. But he lied to me. He left, and now he has another wife and a little baby.
Peter:	I hate my father. I knew nothing, and suddenly one day he came home and told my mother he was leaving. He left for America with a girlfriend and never took any interest in me or my brother. Then, after a year, he came back and now every Tuesday he comes to take us out for a little while. Why does it have to be just on Tuesdays, when I want to go out with my friends?

The children went on sharing their experiences and letting Shirley feel she was not alone in her loss and bereavement. At this stage we did not work on strategies of coping. The session ended with the children telling Shirley what they liked about her.

A Birthday Session

It was Kirsten's eleventh birthday and the group was celebrating it. She was given a ball which passed in the order she chose among the members of the group. On receiving it, each member had to tell her what they liked about her (enhancing her self-concept) and what they wished her on her birthday.

Jill:	I wish you Many Happy Returns and my true wish for you is that you'll be a good mother when you grow up, be good to your children and won't let what happened to the children here happen to them.
Michael:	I wish you good luck in your studies.
Peter:	You have a good imagination, and I think you can find new ways of making your life good in spite of the divorce.
Hilary:	I just love you.
Nina:	You are very beautiful. When you grow up you'll have a very happy family!
Miriam:	I hope you will forgive your parents one day.

After each member had had his or her turn, Kirsten reciprocated by saying what she had felt when she was the centre of all the attention ('I didn't know I could be really liked by anybody and now I see that people care for me!'). The counsellor then lit the candles on the cake and asked the group to look deeply into their flames, asking:

What do the candles remind you of?

Tom: My fourth birthday. I was crying. I don't know why...

Judith: Hanukka; warmth, coloured lights, candles, a happy family.

Jill: Why isn't it like that in every family? Why do families fight? And why do children have to suffer because of it? [*Here the counsellor decided that the next session would deal with Transactional Analysis.*]

Nina: The candles remind me of the cemetery with lots of memorial candles.

Miriam: The candles remind me of a prince dying in India and the people wanting to burn his wife. [*An example of speaking in metaphors?*]

After the cake had been cut by the children, they were told they could have a very short session of play-acting. Miriam asked that her story be chosen, as she had seen a film very much like it.

All right, whom do you choose to be?

Miriam: The princess. 'My life has already been burnt down because the prince has left me. Please don't burn me as well!'

Peter: 'I promise not to burn you if you marry me and give us 12 happy children!'

The children all joined in the dancing and singing at the 'wedding' before discussing their feelings.

Kirsten: I hope all the good wishes I've been given will come true. I always go away from these meetings with a wonderful feeling.

The Transactional Analysis Session

After playing with the puppets and cards, the children had finally understood the various ego-state communications described by TA concepts (see Chapter 14). Dan told of his mother's interrogations regarding his father's girlfriends every time he returned from his weekly visit with his Dad.

Before, I just used to scream at her... now I see it's the 'child' within her... I won't answer her with my child any more. I just explain how much it disturbs me...!

Diana explained:

I can't stand the 'parent' behaviour in my stepfather, mostly because I feel that it's so false. In his heart he doesn't mean the caring things he says. Till now I just used to start getting him mad with my 'child'. Now I'll just try to talk to him with the 'adult' within me. I'm sure things will change now.

In this session, Anna talked about her mother's 'child' ego-state behaviour. This was the first time she had volunteered any intimate information:

I feel as though my mother hates me. She throws shoes at me and beats me with a belt that has buckles. [*She lifted up her shirt and showed her back which was bruised all over.*] My mother is away all night and when I tell her I'm scared of looking after my brother all alone in the house, this is what she does to me.

Another Session

Amy, who had until now been a very silent participant, came in very upset and said:

I'm not speaking to my father any more. I have nothing to say to him when he comes from the city where he lives and I see him slipping money to my big sister but not a penny for me. He just asks boring questions like: 'Well, how are you getting along in your studies?' and we have nothing more to say to each other.

Another child piped up and said that was exactly what was happening with her father. Now that they don't live together, being together seems so empty; they have nothing to say to each other. Diana broke into the conversation:

With me it's just the opposite. I want to live with my father. I can't stand Mum's boyfriend... he stares at me funnily all the time, and he can't make up his mind about Mummy. He comes and goes all the time and can't leave his own children. It makes Mum so nervous.

Here the counsellor introduced the 'developing assertiveness' cards and the children practised speaking to their parents about their troubles by role-playing. First they tried to understand their parent's feelings and then they expressed their own feelings over the matter ('I'm so hurt and feel you love only Vicky when you give her extra pocket money and not me'). The next step was to make suggestions about alternative behaviours; as usual, we discussed our feelings and what insights had been achieved in the group that day.

A Closure Session

Hilary suggested that we sum up by answering the question: 'In what way have I changed since we started this group?'

Nina: I've become more open and can now talk about my feelings even in class and sometimes at home.

Paul: I'm calmer now and less nervous.

Miriam: I think I manage my life much better now... even things that are difficult for me to do or say.

Peter: I think I have more tolerance for other children as well as for my family. I've always had a lump in my throat. I've felt you have all helped me so much. I feel such relief.

PART V

THE CHILD AND THE FAMILY

CHAPTER FOURTEEN

Time and Space for the Individual Child

Indications for Individual Therapy

Some children do better in individual therapy than in groups. These are children who are apprehensive and fearful. Some of them may suffer from emotional disorders or learning disabilities, while others simply refuse to work in groups.

Individual therapy is also used with those children whose parents refuse to allow them to take part in group sessions, lest they reveal family secrets. This is often the case when the divorce has not yet been legally finalised.

Individual therapy is advisable when the child's maladaptive behaviour is related to past misinterpretations of events and is not being corrected by less stressful interactions in the present. A child in the throes of a chaotic family life can benefit from a consistent, predictable therapist (Gardner 1991, Hodges 1986). Various therapies may be used: for example, when a very young child of divorcing parents is faced with unpleasant stressful situations, play therapy may be the treatment of choice (Axline 1969, Moustakes 1959).

Varieties of art and dramatherapy, transactional analysis, storytelling and story-making can be applied to children of all ages. Older children benefit from cognitivley oriented methods, such as subtly tailored reading and writing assignments. It is possible to apply such techniques both to group and individual therapy. Each one of them has diagnostic as well as therapeutic advantages.

Tolerance for Ambiguity and Uncertainty

During transitional periods, one yearns for clarity and certainty: sometimes these are obtainable only if feelings and ideas are pressed into the straitjacket of a 'black or white' perspective.

To prevent such emotional constriction, our aim is to help children, thrown into the unmapped territory of divorce, to gain the flexibility necessary to survive in rapidly changing circumstances.

Tolerance for ambiguity gives us the fortitude to endure unclear situations and consider alternative interpretations. People differ in their thresholds for tolerating such situations, but those thresholds are modifiable and can be raised by repetitive cognitive training.

The following exercises enhance flexibility in perceiving events and thoughts and in solving problems. One way to start raising the 'tolerance for ambiguity threshold' is by practising perceptual discrimination, using ambiguous stimuli. The following pictures are examples of interchangeable figures. The child is helped to accept the fact that there are *no right or wrong answers*. Viewing these pictures and participation in discussions about them help children gain insight into the fact that there are different ideas, opposing viewpoints and alternative ways of seeing reality.

Fish or Swans?

What do you see in the picture?
Count the fish. How many do you see?
How many swans are there in the picture?
Look carefully and count them again.
The picture changes. Sometimes you see swans and sometimes – fish.
Which is the correct answer? Is there a correct answer?

Young Bride or Old Hag?

Tell a story about the woman in the picture.
How old do you think she is?
Look again. Do you think you can see a different woman?
How is that possible?

If I Were...

An additional strategy, adapted from methods suggested by De Bono (1970), enhanced emotional and cognitive flexibility by assigning the children unexpected tasks.

A creative and initially confounding assignment is announced. For example:

Invent a machine that will walk dogs.

The funnier the exercise, the more it helps youngsters to be flexible in their way of thinking and enhances their tolerance for ambiguity and obscurity. As such a machine does not exist, the children must apply their creative energies, not only to inventing the machine but also to taking into account the dog's view of the world. Such exercises introduce the 'inventors' to strange aspects of reality and help them develop tolerance of differing viewpoints. The unexpected assignments presented in each of the following exercises demand a new outlook on reality; a liberated view of conventions and ways of thinking. Creativity is enhanced by the humor inherent in the juxtaposition of two opposites. These unexpected stimuli elicit an inner response that challenges entrenched habits.

If you were a caretaker in the zoo
and wanted to know the elephant's
weight, how would you weigh it?
Please draw!

Invent something to prevent cats
and dogs from fighting.

If you were a teacher, how would
you behave in the classroom? Draw!

Draw a picture showing how you
would improve your body!

Plan a visit to the land of goodies.
Draw and describe!

Invent a sleeping machine!

If you were a policeman, how
would you deal with bad people?
Draw!

Invent a fun-machine!

Invent a machine that puts people into a good mood.

If you wanted to build a house very quickly, how would you do it?

Please invent clothes made of material that has never been used before!

Invent a special patent that turns you into a good students.

How can one turn evil people into
good ones?

If you had a magic umbrella, what
would you do with it?

Invent a space-ship in which people
can live on the moon for as long as
they want.

What About Me? (Questionnaire)

Filling in a questionnaire together with a child (either in writing or out loud)
usually eases the conversation between therapist and child. It also provides
information concerning the child's viewpoint on the divorce. Filling in a questionnaire together with the therapist is also very cathartic. It goes without saying
that the child must be told that any information he or she reveals will be kept
very confidential, and that this promise must be kept.

The following questionnaire is adapted from Allers (1982).

What About Me?

Name...
Date ....
1. How much time has passed since your parents divorce? ....
   ....
2. Have you discussed the divorce with your mother? ....
   ....
3. Have you discussed the divorce with your father?...................................
   ....
4. Have your parents told you why they got divorced?...................................
   ....
5. Do you understand why your parents got divorced? ....
   ....
6. Do you think it was a good idea for your parents to get divorced? ....
   ....
7. Have your parents remarried?
   Mother.....................................Father ....
8. Do you think your parents will remarry?...................................
   Each other.................................Someone else ....
9. Do you blame one, or both, of your parents for divorcing?...........................
   If one, which? ....
10. Do you feel that you are to blame for your parents' divorce? ....
    ....
11. Do you feel that you are partly to blame for your parents' divorce?.........
    ....
12. Do you ever dream of your parents living together or marrying each
    other again? ....
13. Are you interested in learning more about divorce? ....
    ....
14. Are you angry about your parents' divorce? ....
    ....
15. Do you feel you can talk about the divorce with your mother?...............
    Your father? ....
16. What do you think about your parents having new partners? ....
    ....
18. If you live with your mother, do you feel you can contact your father
    whenever you feel like it? ....
    And if you live with your father, do you feel you can contact your
    mother whenever you feel like it?...
19. Do your mother and father talk to each other without fighting?...............
    ....

20. Do you think your mother knows how you feel about the divorce?.........
....

21. Do you think your father knows how you feel about the divorce? ....
....

22. Have you ever spoken to a friend about your parents' divorce?...............
....

23. Do other children usually understand how you feel about your
parents' divorce?..

24. Do your teachers understand what your parents' divorce does to you?..
....

25. Would you like to see the parent with whom you don't live more often?
....

26. Is there anything you enjoy about the divorce?..
....

Parent / Child Projective Stories

Instead of talking directly to the child about his or her problems, we offer
unfinished stories for completion. The following stories are useful for both
diagnostic and therapeutic purposes. They have been adapted from the Despert
projective test (Despert 1979), which is based on psychoanalytic understanding
of the stages of development in the formative years of life, and focuses on the
parent/child relationship.

> Once upon a time there was a daddy bird, a mummy bird and a tiny
> little baby bird. (He was tiny, but he already knew how to fly.) The
> birds lived in a little nest on top of the tree. One night, while the birds
> were asleep, a storm broke out. The branch where their nest perched
> broke into two and the nest fell onto the ground. The birds were very
> alarmed. Daddy bird flew to one tree, Mummy bird flew to another
> tree, but what did the tiny little bird do? ....
> ....
> ....
> ....

Once upon a time there was a sheep who had a baby lamb. The sheep loved the lamb very much. Every evening she gave it warm sweet milk in the field. One day, the sheep brought home a very tiny little lamb and told her lamb: 'Look, I've found this tiny little lamb. He is very hungry, and I must give him some milk. I don't have enough milk for you and for him. You must go and eat some grass'. What did the lamb do? ....
....
....
....

Once there was a boy. This boy had a little elephant, a beautiful elephant, a very sweet one with a long trunk. The boy loved his elephant and played with it every day. One day the boy went for a walk, and when he returned he saw that the elephant had changed. What happened? ....
....
....
....

Once there was a girl who said: 'I'm trembling all over. I've had a terrible dream!' What did she dream about? ....
....
....
....

Mum and Dad had a lovely party on their wedding anniversary. They loved each other very much. In the middle of the party the son got up and went out, all alone, into the garden. Why? ....
....
....
....

Somewhere a little boy sat and whispered: 'I'm so scared, I'm so scared...' What was he scared of? ....
....
....
....

One day a boy went for a beautiful walk with his mother (or father). They enjoyed being together, but when they came home the boy saw that she (or he) had a peculiar and unusual expression on her (or his) face. Why?..
....
....
....

A child came home from school and his mother said to him: 'Don't start doing your homework. I have something very important to tell you.' What did she tell him? ....
....
....
....

Let's say you are walking in the woods and you meet a fairy. The fairy tells you: 'You may have three wishes.' What would you ask for? ....
....
....
....

If you could turn into an animal, which one would you choose to be, and why?...
....
....
....

Transactional Analysis: Ego-States Communication and Games

Transactional Analysis (TA) (Berne 1961) is a rational approach for understanding and reshaping our communication with ourselves and with others. Although originally developed for psychotherapy, we found it very useful as a self-help method for groups and for working with individual children of divorce. Those confused children, whose family break-up has deprived them of coherence and control over the events, need to regain trust. Therefore they can be nourished by the basic assumption of TA – that people can learn to trust themselves, think independently, express themselves freely and make their own choices about the way they respond to external events (James and Jongeward 1971). TA helps them understand the connection between their own feelings, thoughts and behaviours and also see more clearly the motives of their parents' unpredictable behaviour. With some training, the child can learn to replace manipulation or symptoms by directly communicating his or her pain and needs to parents, teachers and peers. The language of TA is simple and descriptive, and thus accessible even to small children.

Everyone says at some time: 'I feel like a child', 'I feel just like my mother/father'. However, one not only *feels,* but also *thinks, considers, decides* and *resolves problems* like a 'child', like an 'adult' or like a 'parent'. It follows that each of us has three permanently resident ego-states: the *'parent'*, the *'adult'* and the *'child'*. Always available, they come to the fore at will, each producing its own unique behaviour. These patterns of behaviour derive from life-experiences. But while the original experience may have been forgotten, the old behaviour-pattern has become internalised. Some patterns may be appropriate and welcome, but others may be outdated, out-of-place and disruptive to social transactions.

The 'Child' Ego-State

The 'child' within us has many faces, created by our early childhood experiences and allowing us to respond to varied life situations spontaneously and emotionally. Among its manifestations are:

The Wild Child – rebellious, cheeky, destructive, aggressive.

The Submissive Child – dependent, anxious, attached, tearful, weak.

The Natural Child – uncensored, curious, impulsive, mischievous, active, playful, creative, sensuous, able to express feelings of pleasure, sadness and happiness.

The 'Parent' Ego-State

The internalized 'parent' has two aspects. The *critical parent* is bossy, full of prejudices about religion, politics and traditions, demands obedience and order, scolds, judges and punishes. The *nurturing parent* worries, takes care, feeds, helps, supports, gives a feeling of security and encourages independence.

The 'Adult' Ego-State

The 'adult' is the part of our personality that uses facts, common sense, reasoning and analysis for making decisions and for carrying them out. It is an 'internal computer' that can guide us in using our feelings so that they don't overwhelm us in the wrong place and at the wrong time.

'Games'

The three ego-states are part of us at every age. Therefore, even children have an 'adult' state that expresses age-appropriate responsible behaviour. We can become aware of the 'parent' or 'child' messages that guide our behaviour and distinguish which ones are suitable in the present and help reach our goals, and which ones are unsuitable and likely to block our progress. Thus, awareness allows us to nurture the creative 'child' within us and not allow dependency or destructive tendencies to overpower us.

Recognising and identifying ego-states can help to clarify the obstacles in relationships between people, when the partners' ego-states clash or block each other. People can learn to enter or exit from each one of the ego-states whenever they want, thus taking responsibility for their lives and their relationships.

The crisis of divorce often reinforces destructive patterns of interaction between family members. In TA language, such patterns are called 'games'. Overt conflicts disguise concealed desires for revenge, competition or self-pity, which entrench the struggles in the family and doom them to endless repetition (Berke and Grant 1983).

The following are common 'games' that spoil relationships between parents and children. Once deciphered, they lose their destructive power and allow much more positive 'adult' patterns to emerge.

YOU'LL BE SORRY IF I DIE (A ONE-SIDED GAME)

Anna is angry with her parents for separating. All her efforts to get them to reunite have failed. The 'punitive and blaming' parental ego-state is then activated: she imagines what will happen if she dies, and how her parents will mourn for her, together.

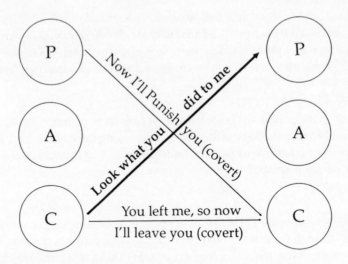

IF YOU DON'T LIKE IT (A GAME FOR TWO)

Christopher is angry with his mother for making him work in both the garden and the house. His mother tries to hide her pain over her husband's leaving her, and hangs on to her son. Christopher, speaking as a 'punitive parent', threatens: 'So I'll go to Dad's'. The mother, in a 'blaming parent' ego-state, feels that Christopher is ungrateful. Instead of listening to him and finding out his feelings, she allows the 'child' in her to lash out: 'If you don't like it here, you can go away immediately!' Neither 'player' intends to carry out the threats, but they succeed in hurting each other just when both need mutual support.

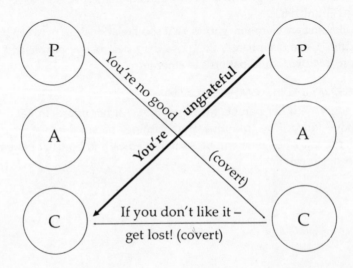

Replacing Games With More Satisfying Interactions

We have devised an illuminating method to teach children the principles of Transactional Analysis by using a large doll with three small dolls under its skirt. Each little doll represents one of the three ego-states. Role-playing with these puppets demonstrates the resolution of conflicts. Once the therapist is sure that the child understands the basics of TA, the child's own problems can be discussed direct, trying to discover the ego-states in his or her own behaviour and in that of others, as illustrated in the following example.

Sarah: Dad's girlfriend treats me with her 'child' ego-state. She curses me and tells me that I'm dirty and I stink. I don't tell Dad because I don't want to hurt his feelings. So I don't go to visit him at all.

Therapist: From which ego-state does your behaviour stem?

Sarah: I think... that it's from the 'parent' in me; I behave towards Dad as though I were his mother. First I worry about him, and then I punish him.

Therapist: Can you think of another kind of reaction, from your 'adult' state?

Sarah: Hmm... maybe I'll just speak to him about all this?

Problems of self-blame and counter-blame are especially suitable for working out through TA This method helps the child reach a deeper understanding of how behaviours arise from ego-states, and how she or he can take responsibility for 'shifting gears' and altering 'games'.

TA can be taught and used both in individual therapy and in group settings. In either case, it is very important to work simultaneously with parents, so that they too will be familiar with ego-state concepts and their implications. At a later stage of therapy, parents and children can meet together and act out ego-states and their variations. For example, when presented with the following problem:

I feel that my son is becoming more and more distant since the divorce. What should I do?

one father was able to imagine three possible responses:

Nurturing Parent ego-state: I'll bring him lots of sweets; I'll buy him whatever he wants.

Mischievous Child ego-state: We'll run away on a trip together, so that nobody will know where we are; we'll have fun.

Adult ego-state: I'll try and find out what he feels,
                                    and I'll also tell him what I feel.
                                    We'll plan how to spend our visits
                                    together.

A child was asked for various responses to the following dilemma:

Your parents are quarrelling – you've heard them say they intend to get
a divorce.

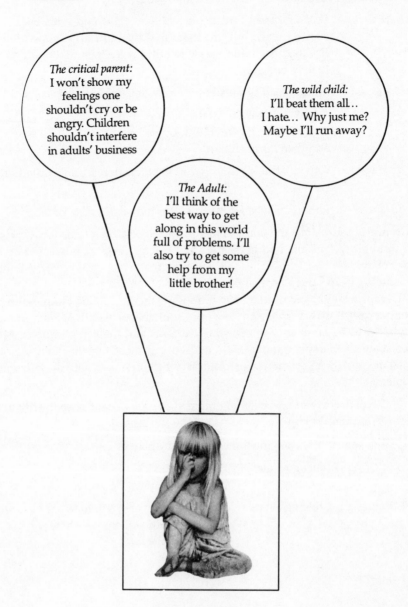

One mother was asked to consider this problem:

> Today I really got kicked in the teeth. Sheila's teacher told me that ever since the divorce, she has been disturbing the teachers and the other children in class. She also hasn't been doing her homework, and often plays truant.

She was able to come up with:

Wild Child ego-state:	I'll kill her!
Worrying Parent ego-state:	Oh, the poor thing. She must be ill; I'll take her to the doctor.
Adult ego-state:	I know Sheila is suffering from the divorce. I'll try to divert her attention from her troubles, and to make life at home pleasant. As time passes, she'll feel better.

After separation and divorce, children tend to align themselves with one 'good' parent (Wallerstein and Kelly 1980, Robson 1982). The following exercise, appropriate in both individual and group therapy, helps children understand what is happening inside themselves.

Children are asked to divide a page into three sections, and to label them as follows:

Mother	Father	Self

Under these headings they are asked, first, to list each person's strengths, and afterwards, each one's weaknesses. We have found that children with a sound understanding of TA can discuss what they have written with insight and balance their relationship with both parents in a realistic manner.

Depict Your World in Lines, Colours and Shapes

We ask the children to create their own world on paper, using shapes, lines and colours. Oaklander (1978) suggests a guided fantasy:

> Close your eyes and go into your space. See your world – what is it like for you? How would you show your world on paper, using only curves and lines and shapes? Think about the colours in your world. How much space would each thing take on your paper? Where will you put yourself in the picture? (p.21)

A child's drawings and paintings give the therapist direct access to her or his inner world, with no need to rationalise or explain. Every component of the drawing reflects the self. The visual translation of the self-concept (not only figure-drawing but every other component as well) is expressed, *inter alia*, by the components' positions on the page, by proportions, by the completeness (or incompleteness) of details, by the stress put onto the crayon or pencil, and by the choice and use of materials (Hesse 1983).

Drawing, like dreaming, often triggers a stream of verbal associations. Here is one example:

> Alistair, age seven, came for therapy because of bizarre behaviour and lack of concentration in the classroom. Because he refused to participate in a group, he was referred to individual therapy. Even in this one-to-one situation, it was difficult to induce him to talk. One day he took up a paintbrush and started painting; he drew a queen, a king climbing a mountain behind her, and a big black bird attacking him. While painting, he began talking, as if to himself.
>
> 'Here, here... he is going to bite him, he's going to tear him to pieces. The king will die. The king is very bad. He ran away from his children. The black hawk will punish him'.
>
> Alistair continued painting hurriedly and murmured quietly:
>
> 'The king is dead, the king is dead!!'
>
> And, as he continued colouring the picture:
>
> 'Why does he leave the children? I hate him!'

Alistair was given the opportunity to express his anger over the fact that his father had left the family and moved out to live with another woman. Keeping within the metaphor, without any additional interpretation, is a very efficient way of working with a child's ambivalent feelings towards parents. The fantasy disguises reality enough to defend children from the anxieties aroused by their anger towards their parents.

The Kinetic Family Drawing

Drawing of family scenes is a powerful activity, that opens 'hidden closets' in the child's life. The drawings often vividly depict the emotional closeness, identifications and aversions existing in the family. Highly guarded secrets, such as physical or sexual abuse, may be exposed.

The following instructions are usually helpful (Burns 1982):

> *Draw a picture of everyone in the family, including you, doing something. Try to draw whole people, not cartoons or stick figures. Remember, make everyone doing something, some kind of action.*

After the drawing has been completed, the following questions may lead to deeper understanding and insight:

- *What do you see in the picture?*

- *What has happened?*

- *What do you notice about the distance between everyone?*

- *Are the people in the picture touching each other?*

- *Are they shutting themselves away from anyone?*

- *Who is facing them?*

- *What are the feelings expressed by the figures in the picture? happiness? sadness? anger? pride? suffering? boredom? stiffness? involvement?*

- *If the family picture were to come to life, what would happen? Who would leave? Who would stay?*

- *What feelings flow from the father?... from the mother?... from yourself? What barriers are there?*

First Release: Rachel

Rachel, age seven, felt very depressed when she learned that her father had a new girl friend with three children. (Her parents had divorced some time previously, and after short-term intervention, Rachel had seemed to be adapting quite well). She refused to talk about the new situation and her behaviour regressed; this was expressed by day-dreaming, thumb-sucking in class and a lack of concentration. She was also unable to express herself verbally to the counsellor. Asked to draw her family doing something, she immediately drew the following picture (Figure 14.1). Without being asked, she said:

Figure 14.1

This is my father buying presents for his girlfriend's three children: clothes, watches, and new shoes in a box. But he buys nothing for me. He doesn't need me any more. The only thing he does is hit me if I don't want to go to see Elaine and her children.

She took another sheet of paper, divided it into two, and continued speaking:

Daddy promised me he wouldn't take me to his girlfriend, but he did and then they forced me to go and visit her sister. I started crying and said I wanted to go home, and Dad's girlfriend started complaining and shouting at him: 'She fucks up everything for us'. Dad took me in his arms and said, 'OK we won't go to her family, we'll just go for a ride'. We got into her car, and we *did go there*. He *did* take me there, he lied to me...

Figure 14.2

Here Rachel burst into tears, as if a dam had been let open. Gently, the counsellor began the therapeutic process.

Identification: Daniel

Seven-year-old Daniel is in the same class as Rachel. His parents have been going through the process of divorce for the last couple of years, mainly because his father has become a drug addict and doesn't support the family. His very young mother has two jobs to help her look after the house and feed her family. Daniel's Kinetic Family Drawing (see Figure 14.3) depicts, on the far left, the father lying in bed. Notice how very small, helpless and meaningless the father seems to Daniel. The second figure in the picture is David, his eleven-year-old brother, who feels very responsible for his father.

This is David, going to ask Dad if he wants any water, or if it was him who took the money from Mum's purse. In the middle is my little baby brother. He is three years old. He likes to play with his car. This is my mother; she is cleaning the house.

Figure 14.3

On the far right, he put himself drawing, because 'I love drawing'. Notice his identification with the father. Even though Daniel is drawing, he is the only one in the picture lying down, much like his father!

The Wrong Approach This Time: Emma

Emma is a twelve-year-old who is experiencing a very traumatic divorce. Her Kinetic Family Drawing (see Figure 14.4) illustrates her regression. It most certainly does not seem like the drawing of a twelve-year-old. The only comment she was willing to make about the picture was:

I'm not drawing my father in the family, and I'm not drawing myself.

Her mother is pictured on the far left. Our asking Emma to draw failed to trigger a conversation concerning her deeper feelings. She was unwilling to add another word.

Figure 14.4

The Family Album

Whether in group, individual or family therapy, children are encouraged to create a family album, which includes parents and their new spouses, all the children in the family and other significant relatives. The album can be created from photos, from pictures cut out of magazines, or by drawing pictures (Naharin 1985). Several suggestions amplify the therapeutic effects of 'the family album':

- *Write a funny caption under each picture*

- *Let each character act (you can write out the parts)*

- *Say whatever you like to the various characters (you can write that down as well)*

- *Two of the characters are conversing with each other. Write the dialogue*

- *Choose colours that express feelings: Draw lines in the appropriate colours between the members of the family*

The Chit-Chat Chips

Following divorce, many children are both suspicious and scared and tend to clam up – just when it is so important for them to express themselves. To help the child relax and gain confidence in the unfamiliar atmosphere of the therapy room, the therapist engages the child in a familiar board game. The activity of rolling dice and moving on a curved path to gain as many chips as possible is usually attractive to children.

The path is divided into a number of sections, some of which are white and some of which are one of three different colours. 'Playing cards', colour-coded to correspond with the coloured squares on the board, are used to trigger verbal and non-verbal expressions, developed according to Gardner (1976). The cards contain open-ended questions for conversation and suggestions for the role-playing of meaningful situations in the child's life. One group also suggests playful activities and 'chit-chat' so as to reduce anxiety and bring some fun into the session.

While playing with the therapist (or with another child or two) the child feels safe to speak of painful subjects that are triggered off by the game. These direct expressions lead to a therapeutic interchange. Our experience shows that this game is a great facilitator of the communication between parents and their children.

Red Cards – Role-Playing

You have a brother and sister who need help. Show how you would help them.	Somebody snatches something from you. Show what you would do.	Pretend you are on the phone. Who are you talking to? What are you saying?
Pretend you are opening a letter you've just received. What's in it?	Imagine your parents as children your age. Pretend to meet them. Speak to them.	Explain to your step-brother that he must not touch your things without permission.
You are a judge. Show how you'd decide the alimony payment for the family.	Show how you look when you are sad, and how you look when you are happy.	You have just written a book about your life. Show how you would sell it.

Scream as loudly as you can. What do you think of people?	Today is your first meeting with your mother's boyfriend. Please play-act it.	You are very angry at someone right next to you. What would you do and say?
Imagine that you've had a very bad dream. Please act out the dream.	Show the stupidest thing a person can do.	Say something insulting to an imaginary person.
Tell your best friend that your parents are getting divorced.	Say something pleasant to an imaginary person.	Play-act an animal you love.

Green Cards – Expressing Feelings

What would you say is the most beautiful thing in the whole world? Why?	A boy's friend leaves him to play with another boy. What does the boy feel?	What is the thing that can hurt a person most of all in the whole wide world? Why?
Dad told you to keep secrets and not to tell anyone. What happens to you?	What do you feel when a teacher favours another child in your class?	Sometimes children are ashamed to tell their parents something. What could it be?
What is the most disappointing thing that has ever happened to you in your family?	Again they didn't keep their promise! Tell them what went through your mind…	Tell about a dream you've had that was filled with feelings.

When did you last cry? What did you cry about?	Mum's new boyfriend comes to your house every evening. What happens to you?	A new brother has been born. What will happen now?
Which part of your body do you like the least? Why?	What is the worst thing that a child can say to his or her father?	What do you feel when you play with someone and he or she cheats?
What scares you most of all?	What does a child feel after swearing at her or his father?	What do you feel when you get up late in the morning?
All the children in the class taunted a child. What happened?	What three things make a person sad?	How do you think crying helps?
What do you think is the ugliest thing in the whole world? Why?	Can you remember something that got you excited?	What kind of things do you like to dream about?
When did you last laugh? Please tell about it.	What is the most important thing that can make a family happy?	What makes a family happy?

What do you like about yourself?	You've heard a fight between your parents. What happened? How do you feel?	What do you feel when you're all alone in the house?
When Mum or dad remarry, children feel that..	Have you ever wanted someone to die? Who? Why?	How do you feel when you learn something sad about someone you love?
What do you feel when you meet a new person?	What is the worst thing a child can say to his or her mother?	What would you do if you had magical powers?
Mother came home very late. What were you afraid of?	What is the most painful thing that could happen to a person? Why?	One boy said that he felt like a ball thrown back and forth between his divorced parents. What did he mean?
What things go through your mind when you can't fall asleep?	What do children feel when they hear, for the first time, that Dad and Mum are getting divorced?	What do you find easiest to ask your parents? What do you find most difficult to ask them?
A child is afraid to talk about something with his father. What doesn't he dare talk about?	All but one of the children in the class were invited to a birthday party? How does that child feel?	Some children are afraid that people will find out 'who they really are'. What are they afraid of?

Purple Cards – 'Chit-Chat'

What present would you like to get for your birthday?	How old is your father? Your mother?	If you could be invisible, but still see and do things, what would you do?
What is the worst thing you could do to someone?	What is worst thing somebody can do to you?	If you had to be turned into somebody else, who would you choose to be?
What is your address?	Tell about three things you are not allowed to do in your home.	Where does your father work?
How many brothers and sisters do you have?	Which animal do you like most in the world? Why?	Who don't you like? Try to find something good to say about her or him.
What do you least like learning at school?	Which is your favourite TV programme?	Tell of pleasant things that happen in the family.
Tell something unusual about your mother.	Of all the things you have in the world, which two do you like the best? Why?	Which subject do you like best in school?

| What would you do if you suddenly got £10,000? | Where does your mother work? | You have just finished writing a book. Give it a name! |

| What traits do you like most in your best friends? | Tell about one of your bad habits! | Who is your favourite teacher this year? |

| What is your favourite colour? | Who is the best teacher you've ever had? Why? | Everybody lies at some time in their life. Tell of the biggest lie you can remember. |

| Pretend you have magical powers and can tell what will happen in the future. Tell what will happen! | Pretend two people are talking about you, and they don't know you are listening. What are they saying? | One girl was the only one not invited to a birthday party. Why do you think she wasn't invited? |

| Pretend you have a magic key that opens all the doors in the world. Which door would you open? | Pretend you have a 'remote control' machine, with which you can control people. Who would you like to control, and what would you make him or her do? | What are the names of your real brothers and sisters? What are the names of your stepbrothers and stepsisters? |

Joint Storytelling

An additional and fun way of working with conflicts and finding new ways to cope is the composition of joint stories or plays. The procedure involves development of a dialogue between therapist and child – the child tells an imaginary story which the therapist can gently direct by intervening at problematic points in the story and redirecting the plot towards positive solutions. Alternatively, the therapist begins a fairy tale or legend (*Once upon a time, far, far away, there was…*) and then invites the child to continue. To arouse the child's interest, the therapist may pretend that they are in a TV or radio studio, conducting an interview.

Karen: I will tell a story about a fish.

              Once upon a time there was a man who went fishing. His son used to shout at him 'What's this? There's no food at home.' The father found a magic fish. The fish said 'Put me back into the sea and I will make magic for you. Big magic. You will have a castle with lots of money.'

              The father came back to the castle. He thought that the fish had lied, because he didn't find the money. He asked his son, 'Where's the money?' The son answered, 'I gave the money to the poor'.

Therapist:	The father went back to the fish and asked for something else. The fish said 'Go home and you'll have a queen, money, food and a very good castle.'
Karen:	He went back to the castle and found that the son had killed the queen and divided the food and money among the poor. The father was very angry and beat his son.
Therapist:	The son said: 'We don't have to think only of ourselves but of others as well. I have left some food for us in the fridge. You bring a queen who will be good to us, whom we will get along with, so we won't be sad. Whoever heard of a castle with a king and prince without a queen?!'

Due to her parents' divorce, Karen had been enduring feelings of loss and deprivation. In her story this experience turns into an exaggerated wish for altruistic philanthropy. The squandering of money and resources gives the child the illusion of control over the sources of the material and emotional nourishment she has been denied, but again she is left feeling deprived of all. The therapist's role is to build a bridge between imagination and reality which will lead the child to an alternative way of thinking. This enables the child to express feelings of anger, deprivation and wishful thinking about satisfaction of real needs.

Letter Writing as Therapy

When communication with a parent reaches a dead end, we suggest a detour: writing a letter not meant to be sent. The therapist may say something like:

> *Let's write a letter to...* [the parent is chosen by the child]. *We won't send the letter. Write anything that comes into your mind.*

The child may write or dictate the letter to the therapist. At the beginning of therapy, the letters often seem to be muddled and jumpy, but as time passes, children manage to express themselves – their frustrations, self-blame, blaming their parents, anger, disappointment and their dreams for the future. As therapy progresses, one may suggest that the child write an imaginary answer, as a means of understanding, adapting to and coping with the situation.

Dad,

I'm writing 'Dad', but I've never ever said 'Dad' to anyone in my life. I don't even know what you look like. There's no picture of you at home. Mum even cut you out of the wedding photos. Only one of your hands has been left. It is resting on Mum's shoulder. I also know that you won't get this letter. I don't even have your address... but I dream of you not at night, but during the day.

Sometimes I'm really mad at you... how could you leave like that... even before I was born... and never, never, never see me? Don't you have a heart? Or don't you think I'm worth wanting? Oh, Dad!!!

When Gail wrote her unknown father's answer, she made him explain his motives and apologise. At the same time, she planned for a joyful meeting between them in the future when he would make up for all the time she had been parted from him.

Even in therapy it was difficult to compensate Gail for all the injustice done her; but the many letters she wrote, and the ensuing discussions, helped release her bottled-up emotions, making it possible for her to adapt to the situation.

Reinforcement

The Self-Awarded Report Card

Towards the end of therapy (both individual and group) it is important to stress the child's emotional as well as cognitive achievements in coping during times of stress. Use of the 'Aims' format serves to strengthen the sense of control the child has over his or her own world.

Aims

1. To make life more meaningful, I can: (*Make the choices that are right for you.*)

    a) Help younger children who are not doing well in their studies.

    b) Start a 'secret gang' to investigate the robberies in the school and in the area we live in.

    c) Find a boy or girl whose parents have started fighting and help him or her with it.

    d) Write a diary or a book about what I have gone through, so that one day it will help others.

2. I have a few more ideas that might help my friends:

    a)

    b)

    c)

3. Because I know I am worthwhile, I am capable of coping and can overcome anything I will have to go through. I am going to cope in a positive and constructive way. (*Write down how you will cope in these situations.*)

    a) At school

    b) With my friends

    c) In the sports club

    d) In my present family

    e) In my 'other' family

    f) In the neighbourhood

    g) With my brothers and sisters

    h) With Grandma and Grandpa.

The Gold Cup

To conclude the therapeutic sessions and acknowledge achievements, the child awards him- or herself a Winner's Cup:

The
Gold Cup
has been awarded to
CHILD'S NAME
for overcoming great difficulties

1. I don't.............................anymore.

2. I can.............................

3. I now understand.............................

4. I.............................

5. I.............................

I still want to overcome:

....

....

CHAPTER FIFTEEN

Counselling Divorced Parents

Group Counselling for Divorced Parents

For most of us, the socialisation process, which we all go through during childhood and adolescence as unavoidable preparation for roles in the adult world, does not provide a script for the ideal 'divorced parent'. If our parents have lived in peace and harmony with each other, there has certainly not been anybody to learn from, and if they have parted, we may not wish to follow whatever example they set.

Groups for divorced parents, led by an expert on human relations in crisis situations, are often the best settings in which to experiment with life in the unknown land of divorce, for many a very peculiar and frightening place. Together with others to whom fate has dealt similar cards, it is possible to map out a future without getting lost. The possibility of learning from others' experiences, together with the need to find a listening ear for the pain and an answer to some of the puzzles, bring many parents to look upon these groups as a 'school' for learning about life after divorce. This learning is even more meaningful if the custodial parent joins a parents' group.

The first principle learned in our groups is that family bonds do not disappear at once and that divorce papers do not drop the curtain on the complex set of relationships with the former spouse. Many divorced people will agree with the following excerpt from a divorced woman's diary (Fuller 1973, p.6):

> ...The judge had pounded his gavel. I could not know what it meant to be divorced, any more than I really could know what it meant to be married on my wedding day. Like any major change in life, divorce does not take place during a ten-minute period on a court calendar. Divorcing is a process, and I found I had to experience all the feelings that go along with it – numbness, anger, fear, confusion, despair – before I had any hope of rediscovering myself and finding a full new life.

The second principle for simultaneously relinquishing the marital role and holding on to the parental role is to find a way to live a new life, satisfying in all its aspects: social, sexual, professional and psychological. The child needs a content and well-balanced parent, not one devoted to martyrdom or to atoning and compensating for real or imagined injustices.

Last, the members learn what the group is for: giving and receiving aid and comfort! The exhaustion which accumulates from perpetual responsibility and loneliness is the major enemy of the single parent. Group members serve both as compassionate listeners and as a real support system, especially since they make themselves available to one another outside of the meetings.

The process of group support can vary, in terms of duration and methods of therapeutic intervention. An example given by Davidoff and Schiller (1983) illustrates a short-term intervention plan that focuses on support and supplying information:

Stage 1:   The first two or three meetings deal with the emotional aspects of the divorce crisis.

Stage 2:   One meeting is devoted to exploring reasons for marriage and divorce.

Stage 3:   A few meetings are utilised for working through grief and bereavement over the 'death of the marriage'.

Stage 4:   Up-to-date information on divorce laws and advice on trials and economic problems is presented.

Stage 5:   This stage deals with children and what being a 'one-parent family' means to each participant.

Stage 6:   The final meetings deal with developing control, independence and personal growth.

A report on group processes found that at Stage 1 the participants tend to share feelings of failure, anger, loss and responsibility, and deal with both apprehensions and the anxieties connected with them. At Stage 2, the relationships between the causes of marriage and the causes of divorce are inspected. This introspection helps release participants from their feelings of personal failure and leads them to a rational examination of themselves, their partners and the relationship system as the whole. The participants become aware that they made their own choices in the past, they continue to do so in the present, and will continue to have control over their lives in the future. The most frequent subjects brought up in parents' group discussions are:

- The difficulty of being a single parent in a society modelled on 'Noah's Ark' ('two by two')
- Organising life so that the divorced parent can find time to be alone or with other adults (this improves the quality of the relationship between parent and children and helps the parent keep his or her sanity!)

- Release from feelings of self-blame and the tendency to over-compensate the children

- Ways of managing on a very limited budget

- Arranging sensible visiting hours with children, to avoid frustration and disappointment for both the parents and the children

- Relationships with the extended family: grandparents, uncles, aunts and other relatives of former spouses, in everyday life and especially during holidays and on birthdays

- Introduction of new partners to the children. How many? When? What are the expectations of the relationships between the children and the new partners?

- Inoculation against social stigma, which produces social ostracism of divorced people and their children

- Building a relationship between the single parent and her or his child(ren).

The Questionnaire: 'About My Child...'

The following questionnaire, developed according to Knight's (1980) guidelines, has been found very useful in early sessions of parents' groups. It encourages conversation in the group, serves as an icebreaker and helps parents understand their feelings and behaviour towards their children.

About My Child...

Please fill out one of these questionnaires for each of your children.

Parent's name ....

Child's name ....

Date ....

1. My child's positive qualities are ....
   ....

2. When my child has difficulties with his/her homework...........................
   ....

3. So that my child has privacy I ....
   ....

4. When I listen to my child...
   ....

5. When I tell my child 'I love you...
   ....

6. I help my child overcome ....
   ....

7. The last time I praised my child...
   ....

---

8. My child smiles when..

....

9. When the other parent of my child is spoken about.................................

....

10. The last time I thanked my child ....

....

11. When my child plays, I..

....

12. Maybe my child does not excel at school, but ....

....

13. My child and I do things together, such as..

....

14. I encourage my child to...

....

15. I show my child affection by

....

16. The tone in which I address my child is principally................................

....

17. In the future, so as to help my child to develop self-respect, I will...........

....

Custody With Empathy

Custody disputes are the most dangerous pitfalls of divorce. To avoid seeing decisions about their children in terms of 'gain and loss' or 'winning and failure', we suggest the following activity. The parents are encouraged to imagine themselves in their children's shoes, entering their world and thoughts, and considering each one's personality, character and temperament, hobbies, skills, talents and weaknesses. What do they like? What do they fear? The custody arrangements can thus be planned from the child's point of view. It is possible to imagine this for babies as well. If there are a number of children, each should be considered separately.

The following questionnaire should be completed by the parents – one for each child – and then by the children themselves.

Custody Arrangements Questionnaire

I know my parents are divorced and not living together. In spite of this, both of them continue to be my parents, to look after me and to love me. They have to make special arrangements to keep things this way. I shall try to help them by expressing my opinions. Of course, not everything I ask for will come true in reality.

To whom do I belong (Who receives all the lawful responsibility over me)?

- Only Daddy
- Only Mummy
- Both of them together.

Where will I live?

- Only with my Mummy
- Only with my Daddy
- I will have a place of my own both at my father's house and at my mother's.

Where will I be during the school year?

- At my Mummy's
- At my Daddy's.

Where will I be at weekends, Christmas and Easter?

- Always in the same house
- I can choose.

Where will I be during the summer holidays?

- At Daddy's
- At Mummy's
- At relatives'
- At friends'
- Somewhere else (where?).

Where will I celebrate my birthdays?

- At Mummy's
- At Daddy's
- Somewhere else (where?).

Who would be in touch with my school: on Parents' Day, to clarify problems and receive reports and for parties and celebrations at school?

- Only Mummy
- Only Daddy
- Both of them together
- Each of them separately, by agreement.

Who will look after me when I'm sick and take me to doctors?
- Mummy
- Daddy
- Someone else (who?).

When something bad happens to me (failure in test, a fight with my friend), I want to tell:
- Both my parents
- Only one of them (Which?)
- One of them, so that he or she will tell the other.

Parents should fill in the questionnaire themselves, and then let each child answer questions either verbally or in writing. A comparison of the two sets of answers enables parents to understand the child's point of view. Taking the answers into account will help real decision-making take place in the light of each parent's conditions and life preferences.

This is the opportunity for parents to explain their decisions to their children, helping them accept those incompatible with their aspirations.

Expectations

Parents should try to imagine their lives five years from now, taking into account the things that are likely to change in the family system: the children's age, the way they spend their time, their needs. Parents might should imagine possible developments in the family status of each of them: remarriage, birth of additional children, change of abode, changes in health, professional life and income.

After divorce, expectation of mutual parenting should be different from those during marriage. What is the difference? Parents may wish to jot down their expectations, as below.

	Married	**Divorced**
Of myself		
Of the other parent		
Of the children		

Joint Groups of Parents and Children

Joint meetings between the separate groups of parents and children may enrich the participants' coping skills. One way to develop mutual insight between parents and children is to introduce a problem and reverse the roles when role-playing. The participant who has raised the problem chooses members of the group to act his or her script in front of everyone – a child acts the part of the parent, and an adult plays the role of the child, while the whole group offers alternative solutions to the dilemma. Apart from the psychological benefit of learning from the behavioural patterns of others and finding alternative solutions to common problems, this procedure allows participants to enjoy themselves and dissipate intergenerational tensions. Newly learned patterns of communication pass from the group into family relationships. The following cards, presenting common problems, may be used as triggers.

My child does his homework late at night.

My child watches TV till late at night. She refuses to listen to me!

My son fights with his big brother exactly when I am trying to rest.

My son demands a lot of money. He
thinks I'm a millionaire.

My parents are afraid for me and
stop me doing lots of things.

I'm always the scapegoat when my
parents are angry about something
that has nothing to do with me.
How should I solve this problem?

I'm dying to talk to my parents, but
they never have time for me.

My parents are quarrelling again. It really disturbs me. What should I do?

 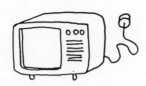

Just when the film begins to be interesting, my mother sends me out of the room!

I punished my child, and now I'm sorry I did it. I don't know how to make up for it.

I know I wasn't right, but such a serious punishment?

My child demands too much pocket-money!

My child has gone down in his studies lately. What should I do? What's happened?

I have a problem. When I ask my child to do something, he never does. He's so lazy.

I can't stand cigarette smoke. All the ads say smoking is dangerous. My Dad smokes and I'm worried about him.

My parents don't come to school
meetings. They work and Dad lives
far away. I understand them, but
I'm ashamed to tell my teacher.
What should I do?

I have a problem – I'm forced to tidy
the room!

I work so hard and the children
don't help me at all.

I come home tired from a trip or
from school, and as soon as I come
in, my mother forces me to tell her
all about it!

I received a bad mark in school.
How should I tell my parents about
it?

I really want a pet, but my parents
won't let me have one.

Family Therapy

We perceive the family as a system composed of sub-systems of parents and children, with each sub-system having different roles (Minuchin 1974). With divorce, however, the parental sub-system is fractured and the balance disturbed. The custodial parent must then withstand the temptation to transfer parental roles to one of the children (usually the first born), and make him or her a 'parental child'. The parental child's attachment to this parent may compensate for loss of contact with the other parent and give this child special privileges and status with regard to younger siblings.

This situation has its advantages both for the parent and for the child, as long as the family system is in the transitional stage (Minuchin 1984). However, prematurely thrusting children into parental roles deprives them of developmentally age-appropriate pleasures and roles and lays upon them burdens of responsibility far above their abilities. They are likely to develop an attitude of 'omnipotence' and entirely escape the control of the parent. Younger siblings are also left to themselves, thereby suffering a threefold loss: loss of contact with the missing parent, loss of intimacy with the remaining parent and loss of closeness with the brother or sister in the child sub-system. All members may benefit from family-therapy, aiming to establish a new balance in the single-parent system.

Assessing Roles Within the Family System

The following methods of evaluating family dynamics may also become means of intervention and change. They are most effective for working with families defined as 'healthy families in temporary crisis'. These methods, as opposed to conventional diagnostic assessment, can be used by the family itself to improve its functioning.

THE FAMILY DRAWING

Kinetic Family Drawing (Burns 1982) reveals the way each family member perceives the rest of the family and his or her place in it (see also Chapter 14). Each member draws a picture of the family, either realistically or symbolically (for example, as animals, coloured geometrical figures or coloured balloons). The discussions following these drawings (*What are the relative positions of each member in the picture? The relative size? Who is missing? Who has been added?*) allow hidden frustrations or expectations within the family to be expressed and, if possible, resolved.

The picture can become a 'Family Sculpture'. Each member of the family is invited to be the 'sculptor' and to arrange the other members of the family in a position that he or she considers suitable. Once this family tableau has been set, the sculptor also freezes, allowing the other members to place him or her according to their own perceptions.

THE 'MISSING PHOTOGRAPH'

The participants are asked to create a pictorial family album (see also Chapter 14). In this case, however, the exercise is taken one step further: each member of the family is asked to imagine an incident that they would have liked to have happened in their family life but which has never actually taken place. Taking each suggestion in turn, the other members of the family start posing for a picture of the event, to the directions given them by the 'photographer', discussing their feelings and thoughts as they do so. When everything is ready, the picture is taken (Naharin 1985). During the discussion, changes in position may be suggested as well as alternative ways of introducing changes in the family.

The Stress Ballet

In her book *Peoplemaking*, Virginia Satir (1972) introduces a method of kinetic sculpting. This is an experiential representation of a stressful situation within the family group. The therapist asks one member to sculpt the picture that occurs when there is a rupture in the family. Other family members then take turns showing their own pictures. This process can be diagnostic as well as therapeutic. The following is a typical example of a family entanglement (pp.155–156).

Let's start with John. He should stand in the middle of the floor, straight and balanced. Then, ask Alice to take his right hand. Ask your firstborn to take his left hand. The second born, Bob, should grasp him around the waist from the front; Trudy should put her arms around his waist from the back. If you have a fourth have him grasp the right knee, a fifth, the left knee. Just keep going until all members of the family have their hands on John. Now, everyone pull gently, slowly but firmly toward themselves until everyone feels the pull. Then freeze.

After a very few seconds, John will begin to feel stretched, uneasy, uncomfortable and miserable. He may even fear he will lose his balance.

John's feelings in this exercise are very similar to what his actual feelings are when too many demands are made on him.

John cannot stay in this position forever. He has to do something. Several choices of action are open. He can decide to endure it and get increasingly more numb until he no longer feels anything. Once this happens he can wait indefinitely. Finally people will just let go, left with the feeling that 'Daddy doesn't care.' Or John can decide to 'bully' his way out by using brute force. Some of the family members might accidentally get slugged or knocked over. Then, as John looks at his family, he can see he has hurt them. He may feel guilty and blame himself for not being able to do what they want or he may blame them for putting burdens on him. The others are likely to feel that Daddy is mean, unloving and hurtful.

Something else John can do is collapse when he feels the pressure. He literally drops to the floor, which represents his solution of becoming sick or helpless. When this happens his family could feel they are bad because they have hurt Daddy. And he could feel angry at them for making him feel weak.

Another choice open to John is to start making deals by bribing and making promises he probably can't keep, but which provide a way out of his misery. In this case John asks each his price for letting go, and the sky is the limit. Whatever they ask for, John will have to say yes, but since the promises aren't real they probably won't be kept. Distrust grows out of this manoeuvre as well as all the other feelings one directs at a promise-breaker.

John still has another choice. At the point of his discomfort he can yell for help to his mother, his therapist, his pastor, the neighbours, a visiting friend. 'Come and get me out of this mess!' And if the one he calls is skilful, powerful or enticing enough, John can be freed. The entrance of an outside party, however, brings new chances for rifts. (This may be how many secret relationships develop outside the family – mistresses, lovers and so on.)

One more choice is open to John. He can be aware that he is an important person to all of those who are asking things of him. He realises that all those people pulling on him are not feeling the same as he is. He can tell all the other family members how he feels and have the confidence that he can ask them for relief and ask for it directly – no hints.

John should now role-play all these ways of getting out of his bind. Then all members of the family can talk about how they felt as this was going on. I think all of them will learn something. Then go through the same procedure with each person having a turn in the centre being pulled.

Bibliotherapy for the Family: Parents' Ordeal

Working with metaphors and stories which portray conflicts helps family members achieve a more objective view of their own situation without increasing their anxiety and guilt. Dealing with their issues projected onto the characters of a story enables them to go through a cathartic process and analyse their own situation from a safe distance. It is very important to choose the appropriate narrative for the family in question in the light of specific therapeutic goals.

Holding-On and Letting-Go

The media has recently brought to the fore the emotional entanglement of custody decisions. One such example is the film *Kramer Versus Kramer* (Corman 1977). Watching this film creates both involvement and detachment at the same time – qualities which enable us to use scenes from the film in our divorce support groups as a means of 'kino-therapy' (similar to the use of stories in biblio-therapy).

The following is a synopsis of the film leading to those scenes that are chosen to highlight the dilemmas of the fighting for custody:

> When Billy was three years old, his mother abruptly left him and his father and disappeared completely from their lives. For a few years his father struggled against all the odds to hold on to his heavy load as sole parent, and, as a result, father and son have forged a strong bond. Now, Billy's mother has re-appeared, claiming custody of the child. His father puts up a fight but loses his case, as the court decrees: 'As between two fit parents, the court must make the best available choice. The court is guided by the best interest of the child and rules that the best interest of the child, who is of tender age, will be served by his return to the mother'.

Such a ruling may still be the in many countries, although more personalised considerations are beginning to influence judges decisions, resulting in more fathers also winning custody. Nevertheless, in contested divorces one of the parents is bound to lose the case.

The scenes from the film, used to trigger responses in the therapeutic group, portray in a personal, vivid and touching manner the father's anguished wait for the court ruling, and the excruciating pain following his realisation that he has lost custody to Billy's mother.

OUT ON A LIMB

Due to high tension during the anxious wait for the court order, parents may be swept into stormy and extreme reactions that are likely to boomerang, causing destruction of property and bitter fights between the couple. At this stage, damage done to the children is bound to be great, especially when one or both of the parents are tempted to turn their children against the other. Nor is the slandering parent immune to the effects of counter-slander by the other parent!

To help families cope with this inevitable stage, we have devised a special process of expression and communication concerning these issues. Parents are asked to compose a script based on their answers to the following questions, and discuss it in the group, protected by the supportive and empathic atmosphere.

- What will happen if I don't get custody of my child?

- How will I be able to look in the mirror – how will I see myself?

- How will I be able to go on having good relationships (or any relationship) with my children, in spite of everything?

- Will I count as a parent?

- Won't my children resent and blame me? Will they ever trust me again?

- What will others (family, friends, for example) think of me?

- What shall I say to each of them?

The majority of children are not aware of their parents' ordeal of fighting for their parental rights in court. Rational explanations don't sink in when the child is in such deep trouble. Children tend to blame the non-custodial parent for abandoning them, and in many instances, the child, as an unwilling accomplice in the parents' struggle, gets a distorted picture of the process. It is especially difficult for children to understand that the final decision over their fate is not in their parents' hands any longer, but has been delegated to the court.

By watching the relevant scenes of the film together, children and parents get the opportunity of mutually experiencing these dilemmas and clearing some of the inevitable misinterpretations. In the relative security of watching Billy's story, children may absorb the following messages:

- Both parents want their children

- Even the non-custodial parent has put up a fight for the child

- The parent who has not been awarded custody is afraid of losing contact with the children.

As part of the therapeutic process children are asked to write a letter to the 'other parent' – the one who was not awarded custody in court – expressing their real or imagined thoughts, feelings and worries. They may offer some suggestions on how they can both hang on to their love even though they no longer live under the same roof. The following exchange between mother and daughter took place after watching the film together:

> Debby had developed a bitter resentment towards her mother, encouraged by her custodial father. She had written: 'I used to think that you never cared about me when you let father win. I thought you had no heart…'. Her mother, with tears in her eyes, pulled out a heavy file full of official letters and documents that told of her long and desperate fight for custody of Debby which she had finally lost, and said: 'I never dared to tell you about all this as I didn't want to spoil your relationship with Dad. Now you know! I've never stopped loving you'.

HAVE I LOST MY CHILD?

Our parents' groups often have mothers and fathers who have lost the primary custody of their children after fierce legal struggles. They inevitabley feel defeated, deflated, angry, and depressed. Phrases such as these often fill the air:

My whole life is over...

I feel as though something is irrevocably broken within me.

I have nothing to live for.

Suicidal and revenge fantasies storm the air. The child may be totally lost in this emotional whirlpool.

At this point, Ted, Billy's father, can become a therapeutic, supportive, identification figure. He is shown to be pulling himself out of his desolation, trying to put the best interests of the child first, and avoiding an open conflict in order to protect the child from having to watch his parents fight over him. Furthermore, Ted takes great pain to project the trust that the boy has developed in him onto the mother.

A crucial issue that is often raised and seldom satisfactorily solved is the way of informing the children of the custody arrangements. How should parents explain to their offspring that one of the parents is going to move out? What should they say? Who shall be the one to break the news? Shall each parent do it separately, or should they both try to handle the situation together?

The 'how' is more important than the 'what'. As is the case with other embarrassing or delicate topics, such as sex or death, every family must find its own way through the mine-fields. However, there is no automatically reliable prescription. It is very important for parents to remember the following suggestions:

- To listen to the child with an open mind, to really hear the questions being asked and to listen for those only hinted at, and to answer their questions truthfully, without concealing one's true emotions, all the while taking care not to overburden the child.

- To avoid piling up all aspects of the painful and complex subject of separation in one conversation. It is better to leave an opening for many further talks between parent and child.

HANDING OVER THE PRECIOUS ONE

To improve the chances of successful parenting by both the 'custodial' and the 'other' parent, each is asked to write a letter describing their child. Each parent has had private times with the children and knows some things that the other does not, and it is very important that these things be brought to the knowledge of the other parent. This letter is likely to be the first step towards changing the pattern of relationships 'in the best interest of the child'. After writing to each other, parents are asked to write a letter to each child, to be read when he or she grows up. The letter should express all the feelings the parents have for the child.

The end of this particular narrative of the Kramer's may be misleading, as this unresolved conflict does not often come to a solution acceptable to both sides. In the Kramer's story, the mother realises the strong father-son bond and decides not to break it. She too makes a personal sacrifice - putting her child's interests before her own. Obviously this is not an ultimate model from a therapeutic point of view, and nor is it a viable model for every family constellation but, nevertheless, the story can become a helpful trigger for discussing alternatives and developing flexibility.

To gain the full benefit of the experience we recommend watching the film twice: once in the divorced parents' group, and the second time together with the children. This may give rise to many questions, which should be aired instead of being bottled up within. We have found that the watching of the 'cinematic story' within the emotional security of the therapeutic group can accelerate the healing affect.

'Parents of the Third Kind'

This story, taken from *Motherhood: The Second Oldest Profession* (Bombeck 1987), is specially suited for all those who claim biological parenthood and/or psychological parenthood (by virtue of birth, adoption or step-parenthood) and who often feel they are victims of their children. It uses well-known elements of folk and fairy-tales. These usually tend to penetrate peoples' hearts and minds trying to solve existential problems without undermining the enormity of their dilemmas.

The protagonists in folk-tales and legends have entered our consciousness as rigid stereotypes whose characteristics we project on various member of the family, such as the king (the father), the stupid son, the evil son, the young 'lucky' son (the prince), and, of course, the evil stepmother. This story, however, uses humour to smash a few stereotypes. Humour releases tension and reduces anxiety. It enables us to relate to a given situation from a distance and from close up simultaneously. The opportunity to be inside and outside a situation at the same time becomes a catalyst for change!

Blended or mixed families are faced with numerous problems concerning their relationships with one another. The following story can highlight few problems when read and discussed by the whole family together.

Hansel and Gretel's Stepmother

Wilma met Hansel and Gretel's father at a woodcutter's convention and it was magic. They liked the same music, the same food, and the same jokes. No one was surprised when, three days later, Wilma gave up her job as a secretary to marry Herb and live with him and his two children in the forest.

From the beginning, Wilma sensed that the children resented her presence. They set the table for three. They coughed on her porridge so she couldn't eat it. And one night they put a dead wolf in her bed.

'Maybe they're getting too much sugar,' she suggested to Herb. 'They seem so hyper.'

'Nonsense,' he said. 'They're just active little children. Try to have a little fun with them.'

Wilma tried. She took them on picnics and they tied her to a tree. She read them little stories and they put a candle under her dress. Finally, Wilma faced the problem realistically. They were the type of children who would kill both parents and make you feel sorry for them because they were orphans.

When she told Herb that something had to be done about their behaviour, he said,

'So, what's your solution?'

'I think we should take them out into the forest and dump them.'

Seeing the horrified look on his face, she said,

'I'm only kidding, Herb. Can't you take a joke?'

But just at that moment, a plan began to form in the warped little minds of Hansel and Gretel – a plan to get Wilma out of their lives for good. They planned an outing in the forest where they purposely got lost. When they returned, they told their father that Wilma had tried to ditch them. The only way they had found their way back was by dropping crumbs.

'She's never liked us,' said Hansel.

'Things were wonderful before she came,' said Gretel.

The next week they once again planned an outing with their stepmother and this time disappeared forever, sealing Wilma's fate.

Several days after their disappearance, the little cottage was overrun with authorities taking fingerprints, looking for clues and questioning Wilma and Herb until they were incoherent.

'There was a Rosemary's Baby quality about those two,' said Wilma.

'Something I couldn't put my finger on.'

'They were just active little children,' Herb growled.

'You weren't here the day they strapped 138 pigeons to their arms and said they were going to fly to South America,' said Wilma. 'I'm telling you, Herb, those kids were weird.'

'Are you saying you're glad they're gone?' asked the inspector.

'I'm saying I think they planned to run away.' said Wilma.

'Then why did we find crumbs of bread a few feet from the house? Is that the act of children who want to stay lost?'

Wilma had no answer. The case against her was too strong for her defense. She was a stepmother who had never displayed any real affection for her two charges. At one point during the trial, when someone mentioned that these two little children would never be seen again, Wilma laughed uncontrollably.

She was sentenced to life in prison for her part in the questionable demise of two small innocent, helpless children.

Wilma was considered quite mad by those around her and incapable of communication. However, one day in the prison library, Wilma's eyes caught sight of a small story on an inside page of The New York Times. It seemed that two small children were being sought for shoving an old woman into an oven. They had conned their way into her home by telling her they had been abandoned in the forest by a wicked stepmother. After they did the old lady in, they ripped off all her treasures and escaped on the back of a white duck.

A chill went through Wilma's body. She wanted to stay where she was forever. She felt safe there.

Remarriage raises high hopes which are very often shattered because of the hostility children show towards the new parent who has entered their lives. The children's anger and fears, due to the loss of the 'perfect' whole family, are projected onto the step-parent. Inspired by anger, fear and suspicion, the children view the stepparent in a threatening and distorted way, the way he or she is symbolised in fairy-tales and other folk- tales. (Stories like Snow-White, Cinderella and Hansel and Gretel have depicted the stepmother as a witch or monster, while modern stories such as *David Copperfield, Fanny and Alexander* and *Lolita* depict the stepfather as a sadist or rapist.)

Under the influence of the stereotype promoted by myth, both children and parents search for the 'evil and cruel syndrome' in the step-parent. Suspicious children test the limits of step-parents by making them go through endless trials, whether by rejecting their attempts at building a relationship or by baiting them.

> Paula was twelve years old when her mother moved to our vicinity from another town. She had started a new life with a man whom she had met at PTA meetings and on school trips. They had both left their previous spouses and Paula's mother had taken the children with her. After reading Wilma's story in a group session, Paula revealed that she was trying her best to drive Alan (her mum's new partner) crazy. She ran around half-naked to get him mad, had the radio on at all hours, came home late, and always interrupted their intimate conversations 'by accident'. The droll way she told this to the group had all the participants in stitches... Later on we role-played the situation. She took turns at acting almost all the roles in the family. According to Paula, this was the 'breakthrough' towards understanding both her mother and Alan (and herself!). It took many more sessions and 'sharings', with the group giving her honest, warm and empathic feedback, before she was able to change her attitude towards her mother and boyfriend, whom she had blamed for breaking up her previous home.

> The children in the group had a code-word: 'Wilma'. Whenever a member started blaming his step-parent for anything and everything that wasn't according to his or her expectations, they used to remind each other: 'Maybe he's doing a "Wilma?"'

If the pranks of Hansel and Gretel, as told by Wilma, seem too exaggerated, a new version of the story can be created – from the daily experiences of the members of a group or family.

Whose Children Are These?

> One Friday, as she was strolling alone down Seventh Avenue, she saw a young, unknown woman holding a child in each hand. She recognised the children.

> Drenched in a cold sweat, fighting the desire to push the woman down and snatch her children, she rushed into the neighbouring deli and burst into tears.

> 'Anything wrong, madam?'

> 'No It's alright.'

'Nothing's right,' he said sternly and handed her a slice of Swiss cheese, waiting expectantly. Then she told him, unwillingly, that she had seen her own children walking down the street with a strange woman, each child holding on to a hand.

'Your children are not yours. They only come to this world through you,' said the grocer.

She stood there helplessly, realising how right he was, but said,

'And history is a hole that gives birth to a hole, that gives birth to a hole.' 'If you want to explain everything with empty words,' shrugged the grocer.

(Eitan 1974)

Incidents such as this occur in the lives of many divorced parents. The pain grows sharper whenever there is danger of losing contact with the children. This text enables the participants to reach deeply into their souls. The need to have exclusive contact with the children – to cling to them, to cut them off from the other parent – arises from the upheaval and destruction resulting from the divorce. When children become the desperate parent's reason for staying alive', that parent will not tolerate their contact with a rival adult.

The mother, who suffers the pain of the loss of her former life, feels threatened when she identifies the 'fingerprints' of 'the other woman's' maternal nurturance. She clings to the children in a desperate attempt to hang on to something constant in her changing world, without considering the children's need to reach an integration of the various parts of their lives – their attachment to their mother and their place in their father's world. The child may begin to show signs of being looked after and nurtured by the father and his new wife. He or she brings back new toys, sweets, clothes, habits and ideas from the 'second home'. The mother – threatened by these clues of 'trespassing' – may resent the fact that her child takes part in another world from which she is shut out. In extreme cases, she may use these objects to fight against the inevitable by refusing to let them enter her home, much to the child's chagrin.

Release

The poet Khalil Gibran has offered gentle advice to overprotective parents, or those who tend to blame themselves for any real or imagined child-rearing mistakes. These insights can guide parents through the maze of divorce:

The Children

Your children are not your children;
They are the sons and daughters of life's longing for itself.
They come through you but not from you,
And though they are with you, yet they belong not to you.
You are the bows from which your children, as living arrows
Are sent forth.
You may strive to be like them,
But seek not to make them like you.
For life goes not backwards, nor tarries with yesterday.

(Gibran 1978)

Recommended Books for Children and Adolescents Experiencing Divorce-Related Crises and Tensions

Children's literature dealing with divorce can be divided into a number of categories.

- Manuals that speak the child's language, and are adapted to his or her level of understanding.
- Books that deal directly with the subject of divorce.
- Books dealing indirectly with subjects of separation and loss through symbols, metaphors or fables. This is done in numerous ways, including exaggeration or humour.
- Poems and stories expressing thoughts and feelings concerning various stressful situations.

Informative Handbooks

These manuals give youngsters advice and deal directly with feelings that might arise as a result of the divorce (anger, blame, fear of abandonment and double loyalty).

Boher, D. (1979) *Coping When Your Family Falls Apart*. New York: Messner.
A 'can do' book that offers suggestions to the problems teenagers face after divorce.

Burt, M. and Burt, R. (1983) *What's Special About Our Stepfamily*. New York: Dolphin Books.
A look at stepfamily living. A must for those youngsters soon to be, or already in, a blended family.

Gardner, R. (1970) *The Boys' and Girls' Book About Divorce*. New York: Vintage Books.
In the introduction to this book, the author says that he gives children advice on how to do a few things by themselves. He suggests that they use it like an encyclopedia; reading it carefully, and then thinking about the things he has said and try act accordingly. He is sure this will help them make their circumstances less difficult.

This book does indeed try to answer, directly, questions such as: 'How can you get along much better with your divorced mother?', 'Who is to blame?', 'How can you know if somebody loves you?' The book suggests ways of solving difficulties or adapting to them. Two very important points are emphasised: (a) that the parents' divorce should not influence the child's self-respect; and (b) that the child is not alone in his or her feelings and reactions to the parents' divorce.

The book deals with the child's feelings (such as anger and blame) and is illustrated by various drawings that depict these feelings. The illustrations in the book are very good and are useful as stimuli for conversations about divorce, within the family or in treatment settings. It is not meant to be read in one sitting, because of the overload of information. Rather, it is advisable to choose a certain problem and to discuss it with the help of the book. Gardner suggests this book as a stimulus for conversations between parents and children.

The book is also meant for children to read on their own (from the sixth grade upwards). It is important that an adult be easily available, so that the child can discuss anything he or she has read.

Goff, B. (1969) *Where is Daddy?* Boston: Beacon Press.
Written to help pre-schoolers cope with grief, loneliness, and confusion after parental separation.

Grollman, E. (1975) *Talking About Divorce.* Boston: Beacon Press.
This book is meant to be read by parents to their younger children – age five and up. With its help, parents can explain to their children why they have decided to get divorced, and that the child is not the cause. The purpose of the book is to give the child a better understanding of the parents' divorce and what it means to him or her. The book focuses on the child's feelings of self-blame and explains: 'You are not the reason that we want to live separately from each other – you are not to blame for the divorce.' However, in the event that the child is hurt, scared or angry because of the new family situation, there are questions in the book that ask the child: 'Are you angry?' 'Are you afraid?' Here the adult reading the book to the child should stop and encourage the child to speak frankly about his or her feelings.

Another point stressed in the book is that divorce is final. 'Whatever you do, it doesn't matter, for mum and dad will not live together any more. We have thought about this for a very long time and our decision is final'. This is a very important point which the child must understand: many children tend to daydream and imagine that their parents will make up and return to each other. Also emphasised is the fact that the parents will continue loving their children and looking after them. It is not enough to *tell* this to the child – he or she has to *feel* it.

Harding, J. (1980) *My Divorce Coloring Book.* Boulder, CO: Childcare Press.
Small children often experience feelings of divided loyalties to their parents: a stimulus for this kind of discussion is to be found in this book. Among the topics are:

- When blame is placed
- When one parent becomes a 'weekend Santa'
- When children are caught in the middle of their parents' fights
- How children can be happy regardless of how their parents feel about each other
- What children can do when they are feeling depressed.

After discussion, children can choose appropriate pages to colour.

Ives, S., Fassler, D. and Lash, M. (1985) *The Divorce Workbook*. Burlington, VT: Waterfront Books.
For parents and children to use together. It explains separation, divorce and remarriage.

LeShan, E. (1978) *What's Going to Happen to Me?* New York: Dolphin Books.
In this book, many questions about divorce are answered: Which parent will I live with? Will a parent remarry?

Magid, L. and Schreibman, W. (1980) *Divorce is...A Kid's Colouring Book*. Gretna, LA: Pelican Co.
With big drawings to colour, this covers 25 divorce-related issues and offers alternative resolutions.

Richards, A. and Willis, I. (1976) *How to Get It Together When Your Parents Are Coming Apart*. New York: Bantam.
A coping book for teens which includes an excellent section on the legal aspects of divorce.

Rofes, E. (1981) *The Kids' Book of Divorce*. Lexington, MA: Lewis Publishing Co.
Children and teenagers share their feelings on divorce.

Sinberg, J. (1978) *Divorce is a Growing-Up Problem*. New York: Avon Books.
A lap book for parents and children, using illustrations to explain separation and divorce.

Sullivan, M. (1988) *The Parent/Child Manual of Divorce*. New York: RGA Publishing Group.
This manual is meant to be read to very young children by their parents. It begins with explanations and instructions for the parents, mainly discussing ways to answer children's questions such as: 'Where will I live after the divorce?' 'Will I still go to the same school?' 'If Daddy is leaving, does that mean he doesn't love me any more?'. Parents who use this guide and read their children the short stories in the book, 'will teach them that the world is not as frightening as they might think and that they are not alone in facing life's difficulties'.

True and Fictional Biographical Stories

Stories dealing with children whose parents have divorced provide opportunities for understanding, identification and catharsis. The child can choose elements in the story that are meaningful to her or him and disregard the rest. In these books, readers encounter other children whose problems are similar to their own and different ways of solving similar difficulties.

Books for Pre-School and Infant School Children (Ages 5–7)

Adams, F. (1973) *Mushy Eggs*. New York: Putnam.
The story of a family managing after divorce.

Berger, T. (1974) *A Friend Can Help*. Chicago, IL: Raintree Publishers Ltd.
This short first-person account tells how important it is for a child to have a peer with whom to discuss important problems such as divorce. Excellent, attractive photographs add meaning to the story.

Boegehold, B. (1985) *Daddy Doesn't Live Here Anymore*. Racine, WI: Western Publishing Co.
Casey, a young girl, is forced to accept the reality of her father's leaving. There are many pictures.

Clifton, L. (1976) *Everett Anderson's Friend*. New York: Holt, Reinhart and Winston.
A child thinks about how his father would have helped him cope with their separation.

Hazen, B.S. (1978) *Two Homes to Live In: A Child's Eye-View of Divorce*. New York: Human Sciences.
Nicki struggles with issues of loyalty, abandonment and anger. Presents divorce issues from a child's viewpoint. A picture book.

Kindred, W. (1973) *Lucky Wilma*. New York: Dial Press.
Presents a good relationship between a visiting father and his daughter.

Lexan, J.M. (1972) *Emily and the Klunky Baby and the Next Door Dog*. New York: Dial Press.
A story about a child who feels neglected after her parents divorce.

Mayle, P. (1980) *Divorce Can Happen to the Nicest People*. New York: MacMillan.
An illustrated handbook that deals with divorce and a child's new life with one parent.

Rogers, H.S. (1975) *Morris and his Brave Lion*. New York: McGraw-Hill.
Has an unrealistic ending, but is otherwise a good treatment of divorce.

Thomas I. (1976) *Eliza's Daddy*. New York: Harcourt Brace Jovanovich.
Deals with remarriage.

Zindel, P. (1975) *I Love My Mother*. New York: Harper and Row.
A small boy talks about having a single parent (his mother).

Books for Junior and Middle School Children (Ages 8–12)

Anchor, C. (1975) *Last Night I Saw Andromeda*. New York: Walch.
A story about an eleven-year-old girl trying to win her divorced father's love.

Bawden, N.M.K. (1969) *The Runaway Summer*. Philadelphia, PA: J.B. Lippincott Co.
Discusses many aspects of divorce: displacement of aggression; meanings of friendship; honesty/dishonesty; parental rejection; living in the home of relatives. The story provides a realistic picture of an angry, frustrated girl who, one summer, attempts to deal with her feelings and problems by running away from them. Her experiences help her mature to the point where she recognises that problems can be solved only by facing unpleasant situations and dealing with them and that 'things can change all the time and it isn't always sad'. The spirit of adventure that pervades the story increases reader appeal. It is also available in Braille.

Blue, R. (1972) *A Month of Sundays.* New York: Franklin Watts.
A boy struggles to accept a move to New York with his mother after a divorce.

Blume, J. (1972) *It's Not the End of the World.* New York: Bradbury Press.
This book addresses the problem of reconciliation fantasies, as Karen, age eleven, tries to understand the divorce. Her goal is to bring her parents back together.

Brenenfeld, F. (1980) *Mum and Dad are Getting a Divorce!* Minnesota: EMC Corporation.
The story of a boy and girl who tell 'how it is'. The purpose of the book is to help children acknowledge and communicate feelings about the divorce.

Cleaver, V. and Cleaver, B. (1968) *Lady Ellen Grae.* New York: J.B. Lippincott. An intelligent eleven-year-old girl lives with her father during the summer, but must adjust to living with other relatives during the school year.

Clymer, E. (1973) *Lucie Was There.* New York: Holt, Rinehart and Winston.
A boy searches for security after his father leaves; the story takes place in a city.

Ewing, K. (1975) *A Private Matter.* New York: Harcourt Brace Jovanovich.
Marcy 'adopts' an elderly man in order to give and receive affection, and finally accepts her parents' divorce.

Hunter, E. (1976) *Me and Mr Stenner.* New York: Atheneum.
When Mum remarries, Abby learns she can love both her stepfather and her real father.

Newfield, M. (1975) *A Book for Jodan.* New York: Atheneum.
Jodan is shaken by parental separation. Didn't they love her anymore? Was she to blame?

Park, B. (1981) *Don't Make Me Smile.* New York: Knopf.
Charles refuses to attend school and runs away after the divorce. His parents are insensitive to his anger.

Seuling, B. (1985) *What Kind of Family is This?* Racine, WI: Western Publishing Co.
Jeff moves into a new house after his mother remarries. He must adjust to living with his stepfather.

Books for Younger Secondary and Upper School Children (Ages 12–15)

Alexander, A. (1975) *To Live a Lie.* New York: Atheneum.
A girl imagines she is unloved and unwanted, and gives herself a new identity and name.

Arundel, H. (1972) *A Family Failing.* Philadelphia, PA: Thomas Nelson.
An eighteen-year-old girl experiences the disintegration of her family and learns to view her parents as people apart from herself.

Barnwell, R.D. (1972) *Shadow on the Water.* New York: David McKay.
A thirteen-year-old girl responds to the painful situation between her parents.

Bradbury, B. (1967) *The Blue Years.* New York: Ives Washburn.
A seventeen-year-old girl believes at first that she has caused her parents to divorce. She goes away to college rather than deal with her problems with her mother.

Berger, T. (1976) *How Does It Feel When Your Parents Get Divorced?* New York: Messner.
A girl deals with anger, fear and sadness. The book includes pictures to express feelings.

Brooks, J. (1973) *Uncle Mike's Boy.* New York: Harper and Row Publishers.
Deals with divorce and guilt feelings, a father's alcoholism, acceptance of change, resistance to change, death of a sibling, mental illness and stages of mourning. In this compassionate story, Uncle Mike represents a calm and steady influence in Pudge's confused, guilt-ridden life. Pudge's parents, who appear to be emotionally unstable, do not listen to him or give him the support and love he needs, particularly during times of stress. Because of Uncle Mike's love and Pudge's ability to see that others have adjusted to one-parent homes, he is able to place stressful situations in perspective and accept them.

Holland, I. (1973) *Heads You Win, Tails I Lose.* Philadelphia, PA: J.B. Lippincott.
The story of an overweight fifteen-year-old whose parents battle constantly and finally separate.

Klein, N. (1974) *Taking Sides.* New York: Pantheon.
Nell adjusts to life with her father and brother after divorce.

Mann, P. (1973) *My Dad Lives in a Downtown Hotel.* New York: Scholastic Press.
A boy feels that he is responsible for his parents' divorce and shows how he deals with these feelings.

Books for Teenagers

Cameron, E. (1975) *To the Green Mountain.* New York: Dutton.
Kath lives with her mother, who makes the painful decision to divorce her Dad.

Eyerly, J. (1964) *The World of Ellen March.* Philadelphia, PA: J.B. Lippincott Co.
Fifteen year-old Ellen March overhears her parents discussing plans for divorce. Ellen, unaware until then of any unhappiness between them, feels shocked and somehow responsible for what has happened. It is decided that Ellen, her mother and her six-year-old sister, Peggy, will move from New York City to a smaller town. On the train to her new home Ellen meets Alex, a boy who intrigues her. She soon makes new friends in school, but carefully conceals her parents' separation and their divorce plans. When Ellen meets Alex again, she is disappointed to learn that he is dating another girl. Still unable to accept the reality of her parents' separation, Ellen schemes to reunite them by running away and taking Peggy with her. However, an automobile accident and other unexpected incidents nearly cause Ellen's death. When Alex visits Ellen in the hospital, he helps her realise that her parents' divorce is inevitable, but in no way her fault.

List, J. (1980) *The Day the Loving Stopped: A Daughter's View of Her Parents' Divorce.* New York: Seaview.
Julie tells how she felt when her father left and how she copes with having to live two lives – with Mum and Dad.

Tyler, A. (1982) *Dinner at the Homesick Restaurant.* New York: Knopf.
Two brothers and their sister, deserted by their father, are raised by their angry mother.

References

Allers, R. (1982) *Divorced Children and the School*. New Jersey: Princeton Books.

Axline, V. (1969) *Play Therapy*. New York: Ballantine Books.

Ayalon, O. (1978) *C.O.P.E. Emergency Kit*. Haifa: Haifa University Publishing (Hebrew)

Ayalon, O. (1979a) 'Is death a proper subject for the classroom?' *The International Journal of Social Psychiatry*. 25:4, 252–257.

Ayalon, O. (1979b) 'Community Oriented Preparation for Emergency: C.O.P.E.' *Death Education* 3:4, 222–244.

Ayalon, O. (1983) *Precarious Balance: Coping With Stress in the Family*. Tel Aviv: Sifriat Poalim (Hebrew).

Ayalon, O. (1987) 'Living in a dangerous environment' (with Van Tassel'). In M. Brassard, R. Germain and S. Hart (eds.) *Psychological Maltreatment of Children and Youth*. New York: Pergamon.

Ayalon, O. (1992) *Rescue! – Helping Children Cope with Stress*. Ellicott City: Chevron Publishing Corporation.

Ayalon, O. (1993) 'Post Traumatic Stress recovery'. In J. Wilson and B. Raphael, *International Handbook of Traumatic Stress Syndromes*. New York: Plenum Press.

Ayalon, O. and Lahad, M. (1990) *Life on the Edge: Stress and Coping in High-Risk Situations*. Haifa: Nord Publication (Hebrew).

Ayalon, O. and Lahad, M. (1992) *Looking Ahead at Life's Options: Suicide Prevention*. Haifa: Nord Publications (Hebrew).

Ben-Ezer, E. (1979) *Offerit Blofferit* (appears in text as 'Tilly Tall-Tale'). Tel Aviv: Yavneh (Hebrew).

Berke, M. and Grant, J. (1983) *Games Divorced People Play*. New York: Prentice Hall.

Berne, E. (1961) *Transactional Analysis in Psychotherapy*. New York: Grove Press.

Bessell, H. (1976) *Methods in Human Development: Theory Manual*. California: Human Development Training Institute Inc.

Bettelheim, B. (1976) *The Uses of Enchantment: The Meaning and Importance of Fairy Tales*. Harmondsworth: Penguin Books.

Bettelheim, B. and Zelan, K. (1982) *On Learning to Read: The Child's Fascination with Meaning*. New York: Vintage Books.

Bombeck, E. (1987) *Motherhood, The Second Oldest Profession*. New York: Dell.

Breznitz, S. (ed.) (1984) *The Denial of Stress*. New York: International University Press.

Buber, M. (1965) *The Knowledge of Man*. New York: Harper and Row Publishers Inc.

Burla, O. (1968) 'Zebra Zebroni'. In O. Burla *Inside the Outside*. Tel-Aviv: Am-Oved (Hebrew).

Burns, R. (1982) *Self-Growth in Families Kinetic Family Drawing (K.F.D.): Research and Application*. New York: Bruner/Mazel.

Caplan, G. (1964) *Principles of Preventive Psychiatry*. New York: Basic Books.

Cohen, S. (1985) 'Divorce mediation: An introduction'. *Journal of Psychotherapy and the Family*, 1(3) 69–84.

Colton, H. (1988) *Touch Therapy*. New York: Kensington Publishing Corporation.

Corman, A. (1977) *Kramer Versus Kramer*. New York: Signet.

Coue, E. (1922) *Self-Mastery*. London: George Allen and Unwin.

Davidoff, I. and Schiller, M. (1983) 'The divorce workshop as crisis intervention: A practical model.' *Journal of Divorce*, 6(4).

De Bono, E. (1970) *The Dog-Exercising Machine*. Harmondsworth: Penguin Books.

Despert, J.L. (1979) 'The Despert Fable Test'. In G. Parson (ed.) *Emotional Disorders of Children*. New York: Norton.

Dunne, C. Bruggen, P. and O'Brian, C. (1982) 'Touch and action in group therapy of younger adolescents'. *Journal of Adolescents*, 5, 31–38.

Einat, A. (1980) *Separation*. Tel-Aviv: Eked (Hebrew).

Eitan, R. (1974) *Chest and Chests*. Tel Aviv: Am Oved (Hebrew).

Ellis, A. (1991) The revised ABCs of rational-emotive therapy, *Journal of Rational-Emotive Cognitive Therapy* 9(3) 39–172.

Felner, R.D., Farber, S.S. and Primavera, J. (1980) 'Children of Divorce, Stressful life events and transitions: A framework for preventive efforts'. In R.H. Price, R.F. Ketterer, B.C. Bader and J. Monahan (eds) *Prevention in Mental Health: Research, Policy and Practice*. Beverley Hills, CA: Sage.

Flasher, A. (1984) *Existential Problems Faced by Children Living in Israel and their Reflection in the Basal Readers in Use in the Primary Grades*. A Thesis Submitted for the M.A. Degree. University of Haifa, School of Education (Hebrew).

Francke, L.B. (1983) *Growing Up Divorced*. New York: Fawcett Crest.

Frankenstein, C. (1966) *The Roots of the Ego*. Baltimore: Williams and Wilkins Co.

Frankenstein, C. (1970) *Impaired Intelligence*. New York: Gordon and Breach.

Frankenstein, C. (1981) *They Think Again*. New York: Van Nostrand Reinhold Co.

Fuller, Y. (1973) *Space: The Scrapbook of My Divorce*. Connecticut: Fawcett.

Gardner, R.A. (1976) *Psychotherapy with Children of Divorce*. New York: Jason Aronson.

Gardner, R.A. (1991) *The Parents' Book about Divorce* (revised edition). London: Bantam Books.

Gersie, A. (1984) 'Have your dream of life come true: Myth-making'. *Journal of the British Association for Dramatherapy*, 7(2) 3–11. March.

Gersie, A. (1991) *Storymaking in Bereavement*. London: Jessica Kingsley Publishers.

Gersie, A. and King, N. (1990) *Storymaking in Education and Therapy*. London: Jessica Kingsley Publishers.

Gibran, K.G. (1978) *The Prophet*. Tel-Aviv: Tamus Publications.

Goetting, A. (1981) 'Divorce outcome research'. *Journal of Family Issues*, 2, 350–378.

Goldstein, J., Freud, A. and Solnit, A. (1973) *Beyond the Best Interests of the Child*. New York: The Free Press.

Gottlieb, E. and Shimron, D. (1982) *Crossroads: A Hebrew Guide to Values Clarification*. Ramot, Tel-Aviv University (Hebrew).

Gwynn, C.A. and Brantley, H.T. (1987) 'Effects on a divorce group intervention for elementary school children'. *Psychology in the Schools*, 24, April.

Hammond, J.M. (1981) 'Loss of the family unit: counseling groups to help kids'. *The Personnel and Guidance Journal*, 59, (Feb) 392–396.

Haynes, J.M. (1981) *Divorce Mediation*. New York: Springer Publishing Co.

Hesse, P. (1983) *Education and Therapy Through Creativity and Art Therapy*. Haifa University, School of Education, Department of Training and Services in Education (Hebrew).

Hetherington, E.M. (1979) 'Divorce: A child's perspective'. *American Psychologist*, 34, 851–858.

Hetherington, E.M. (1981) *Parent-Child Interaction: Theory, Research and Prospects*. New York: Academic Press.

Hetherington, E.M., Cox, M. and Cox, R. (1982) 'Effects of divorce on parents and children'. In M.E. Lamb (ed.) *Nontraditional Families: Parenting and Child Development*, pp.233–288. Hillsdale, N.J.: Erlbaum.

Hodges, W.F. (1986) *Intervention for Children of Divorce: Custody, Access and Psychotherapy*. New York: John Wiley and Sons.

Holmes, T.M. and Raye, R.H. (1967) 'The Social Readjustment Rating Scale'. *Journal of Psychosomatic Research*, 11, 213–218.

Howe, L. and Howe, M. (1975) *Personalizing Education: Values Clarification and Beyond*. New York: Hart Publications.

James, M. and Jongeward, D. (1971) *Born to Win: Transactional Analysis with Gestalt Experiments*. New York: Signet.

Jennings, S. (1986) *Creative Drama in Groupwork*. London: Winslow Press.

Jennings, S. (1990) *Dramatherapy with Families, Groups and Individuals*. London: Jessica Kingsley Publishers.

Johnston, J.R. and Campbell, L.E. (1988) *Impasse of Divorce*. London: Collier Macmillan Publishers.

Kanner, A.D., Coyne, J.C., Schafer, C. and Lazarus, R.S. (1981) 'Comparison of two modes of stress measurements'. *Journal of Behavioural Medicine*, 4(1) 1–38.

Keat, D.B. (1979) *Multimodal Therapy With Children*. Elmsford, New York: Pergamon.

Knight, B. (1980) *Enjoying Single Parenthood*. Toronto: Van Nostram.

Kubovi, D. (1992) *Bibliotherapy: Literature, Education, and Mental Health*. Jerusalem: Magnes (Hebrew).

Lahad, M. (1984) *Evaluation of a Multimodal Program to Strengthen the Coping of Children and Teachers under Stress of Shelling*. PhD dissertation. San Raphael: C. P.U.

Lahad, M. (1992) 'Coping resources through storytelling'. In S. Jennings (ed.) *Drama Therapy: Theory and Practice*. London: Routledge.

Lahad, M. and Ayalon, O. (1993) *On Life and Death*. Haifa: Nord Publication (Hebrew).

Lazarus, A. (1978) *In the Mind's Eye: The Power of Imagery for Personal Enrichment*. New York: The Guilford Press.

Lesowitz, M., Kalter, N., Pickar, J., Chethik, M. and Schaefer, M. (1987) 'School-based developmental facilitation groups for children of divorce: Issues of group process'. *Psychotherapy*, 24(1) 90–95.

Liebmann, M. (1986) *Art Therapy for Groups*. London: Croom Helm Ltd.

Meichenbaum, D. (1983) *Coping with Stress*. London: Century Publishing.

Meichenbaum, D. (1985) *Stress Inoculation Training*. New York: Perrgamon Press.

Minuchin, S. (1974) *Families and Family Therapy*. Cambridge: Harvard University Press.

Minuchin, S. (1984) *Family Kaleidoscope*. Cambridge and London: Harvard University Press.

Morris, K.T. and Cinnamon, K.M. (1975) *A Handbook of Non- Verbal Group Exercises*. San Diego, CA: Applied Skills Press.

Morris, K.T. and Cinnamon, K.M. (1983) *A Handbook of Verbal Group Expression*. San Diego, CA: Applied Skills Press.

Moustakas, C. (1959) *Psychotherapy with Children*. New York: Ballentine.

Naharin, E. (1985) *A Stage Instead of a Couch: Psychodramas*. Tel-Aviv: Tcherikover Pubs. (Hebrew).

Noy, S. (1991) *Combat Stress Reactions*. Tel Aviv: Ministry of Defense (Hebrew).

Oaklander, V. (1978) *Windows to Our Children*. Utah: Real People Press.

Omizo, M.M. and Omizo, S.A. (1988) 'The effects of participation in group counseling sessions on self-esteem and locus of control among adolescents from divorced families'. *The School Counselor*, 36(1) 54–60.

Palomares, U. and Ball, G. (1980) *Grounds for Growth*. California: Human Development.

Peale, N. (1982) *Positive Imagining*. New York: Fawcett Crest.

Pelletier, K. (1987) *Mind as Healer, Mind as Slayer*. New York: Delta.

Pfeifer, G. and Abrams, L. (1984) 'School-based discussion groups for children of divorce: A pilot program'. *Group Counselling*, 8(4) Winter.

Raviv, A. and Katzenelson, E. (1986) *Crisis and Change in the Life of The Child and His Family*. Tel-Aviv: Maariv (Hebrew).

Ricci, J. (1980) *Mom's House, Dad's House: Making Shared Custody Work*. New York: Collier Books.

Robson, B.A. (1982) 'A developmental approach to the treatment of divorcing parents'. In L. Messinger (ed.) *Therapy with Remarriage Families*. Rockville, MD: Aspen Systems.

Rosenthal, R. and Jacobson, L. (1968) *Pygmalion in the Classroom*. New York: Holt, Reinhart, Winston.

Santrock, J.W. and Warshak, R.A. (1979) 'Father custody and social development in boys and girls'. *Journal of Social Psychology*, 35, 112–125.

Satir, V. (1972) *Peoplemaking*. Palo Alto: Science and Behaviour Books.

Seligman, M. (1975) *Helplessness-Depression, Development and Death*. San Francisco: Freeman.

Selye, H. (1966) *The Stress of Life*. New York: McGraw-Hill.

Sharlene, A.W., Fogas, S.D. and Sandler, I.N. (1984) 'Environmental change and children of divorce'. In H.J. Humphrey *Stress in Childhood*. New York: AMS Press.

Shechtman, Z. (1980) 'Values Clarification as a System for Strengthening the Individual'. *Chavat Daat*, 13, 57–66 (Hebrew).

Shenhar-Elroi, A. (1986) *The Folk-Tale for the Child*. Haifa: Haifa University (Hebrew).

Shiryon, M. (1978) 'Literatherapy, Theory and Application'. In R. Rubin (ed) *Bibliotherapy Sourcebook*. New York: Oryx Press.

Simon, S.B. (1974) 'Please touch: How to combat skin hunger in our schools'. *Scholastic Teacher Magazine (Junior/Senior High School Teachers' Edition)* October 22–25.

Simon, S.B., Howe, L.W. and Kirschenbaum, H. (1978) *Values Clarification. A Handbook of Practical Strategies for Teachers and Students*. New York: Dodd, Mead and Co.

Simon, S.B. and O'Rourke, R.D. (1977) *Developing Values with Exceptional Children*. New Jersey: Prentice-Hall, Inc.

Simonton, C., Matthews-Simonton, S. and Creighton, J. (1980) *Getting Well Again*. New York: Bantam Books.

Smilansky, S. and Weisman, T. (1981) 'Cognitive, social and emotional adjustment of elementary school children of divorced parents'. *Studies in Education*, 31, 27–44, University of Haifa, School of Education. (Hebrew).

Snunit, M. (1984) *The Soul-Bird*. Tel-Aviv: Massadah (Hebrew).

Sonnerstein-Schneider, M. and Baird, K.L. (1986) 'Group counseling children of divorce in the elementary schools: Understanding process and technique'. *Personnel and Guidance Journal*, 59, 88–91.

Soskis, D. and Ayalon, O. (1986) 'A Six-Year Follow-up of Hostage Victims'. *Terrorism*, 7(4) 411–415.

Symonds, M. (1980) 'The second injury to victims'. *Evaluation and Change* (Special Issue) 36–39.

Thompson, C.L., Cole, D., Kammer, P. and Barker, R. (1984) 'Support groups for children of divorced parents'. *Elementary School Guidance and Counseling*, 19(1) 88–89.

Tiktin, E.A. and Cobb, C. (1983) 'Treating post-divorce adjustment in latency age children: A focused group paradigm'. *Social Work with Groups*, 6(2).

Wallerstein, J.S. (1983) 'Children of divorce: Stress and developmental tasks'. In N. Garmezy and M. Rutter (eds.) *Stress, Coping and Development in Children*, 265–302. New York: McGraw-Hill.

Wallerstein, J.S. and Blakeslee, S. (1989) *Second Chances: Men, Women and Children a Decade After Divorce*. New York: Ticknnor and Fields.

Wallerstein, J.S. and Kelly, J.B. (1979) 'Children and divorce: A review'. *Social Work*, 24, 468–475.

Wallerstein, J.S. and Kelly, J.B. (1980) *Surviving the Breakup: How Children and Parents Cope with Divorce*. New York: Basic Books.

Ware, C. (1983) *Sharing Parenthood After Divorce*. New York: Bantam Books.

Wheeler, D. and Janis, I. (1980) *A Practical Guide for Making Decisions*. New York: The Free Press.

Wheeler, M. (1980) *Divided Children*. New York: Penguin Books.

Yalom, I.D. (1985) *The Theory and Practice of Group Psychotherapy (Third Edition)* New York: Basic Books.

Zaidel, S. (1991) *Divorce with Respect*. Haifa: Divorce with Respect Publications.

Zarchi, N. (1979) *Don't Throw Nani Out*. Tel-Aviv: Sifriat Poalim (Hebrew).

Further Reading

Ahrons, C.R. and Rodgers, R.H. (1987) *Divorced Families: A Multidisciplinary Developmental View*. New York: W.W. Norton and Company.

Anthony, E.J. (1974) 'Children at risk from divorce: A review'. In E.J. Anthony and C. Koupernick (eds.) *The Child in his Family: Children at Psychiatric Risk* (Vol.3) New York: John Wiley and Sons.

Berg, B. (1986) 'The changing family game: Cognitive-behavioural intervention for children of divorce'. In C.E. Schaefer and S.E. Reid (eds.) *Therapeutic Use of Childhood Games*. New York: John Wiley and Sons, Inc.

Blechman, E. (1974) 'The family contract game'. *The Family Co-Ordinator*, 269–281.

Block, J.H., Block, J. and Gjerde, P.F. (1986) 'The personality of children prior to divorce: A prospective study'. *Child Development*, 57, 827–840.

Bloom, B.L., Hodges, W.F., Kern, M.B. and McFaddin, S.C. (1985) 'A preventive intervention programme for the newly separated: Final evaluations'. *American Journal of Orthopsychiatry*, 55, 9–26.

Bonkowski, S.E., Bequette, S.Q. and Boomhower, S. (1984) 'A group design to help children adjust to parental divorce'. *Social Casework*, 65, 131–137.

Brannen, J. and Collard, J. (1982) *Marriages in Trouble*. London: Tavistock Publications.

Cadoret, R.J. and Caine, C. (1980) 'Sex differences in predictors of antisocial behaviour in adoptees'. *Archives of General Psychiatry*, 37, 1171–1175.

Cantor, D.W. (1977) 'School-based groups for children of divorce'. *Journal of Divorce*, 1(2) 183–187.

Cantor, D.W. (1979) 'Divorce: A view from the children'. *Journal of Divorce*, 3, 353–361.

Cantor, D.W. (1982) 'The psychologist as a child advocate with divorcing families'. *Journal of Divorce*, 6, 77–86.

Cantor, D.W. and Drake, E.A. (1983) *Divorced Parents and Their Children. A Guide for Mental Health Professionals*. New York: Springer Publishing Co.

Cantrell, R.G. (1986) 'Adjustment to divorce: Three components to assist children'. *Elementary School Guidance and Counselling*. February 20 (3).

Capy, M. (1981) *Story-telling as a Process in Education and Therapy*. Haifa University.

Cebollero, A.M., Cruise, K. and Stollack, G. (1987) 'The long-term effects of divorce: Mothers and children in concurrent support groups'. *Journal of Divorce*, 10, 219–227.

Derdyn, A.P. (1980) 'Divorce and children: Clinical interventions'. *Psychiatric Annals*, 10(4) 22–47.

Douglas, J.W., Ross, J.M. and Simpson, H.R. (1968) *All Our Future*. London: Peter Davies.

Drake, E.A. (1979) 'Helping the school cope with children of divorce'. *Journal of Divorce*, 3, 69–75.

Effron, A. (1980) 'Children and divorce: Help from an elementary school'. *Social Casework*, 61, 305–312.

Farber, S.S., Felner, R.D. and Primavera, J. (1985) 'Parental separation/divorce and adolescents: An examination of factors mediating adaption'. *American Journal of Community Psychology*, 13, 171–185.

Finch, A.J. and Kendall, P.S. (1979) 'Impulsive behaviours: From research to treatment'. In A.J. Finch and P.S. Kendall (eds.) *Clinical Treatment and Research in Child Psychopathology*. New York: Spectrum.

Freud, S. (1976) *Jokes and their Relation to the Unconscious*. The Pelican Freud Library Vol. 6. New York: Penguin Books (Original Work Published 1905).

Gardner, R.A. (1975) *Psychotherapeutic Approaches to the Resistant Child*. New York: Aronson.

Gerler, E.R. (1980) 'Longitudinal study of multimodal approaches to small group psychological education'. *School Counselor*, 27, 184–190.

Gerler, E.R. and Locke, D.C. (1980) 'Multimodal education: A model with promise'. *Phi Delta Kappan*, 62, 214–215.

Glick, P. (1979) 'Children of divorced parents in demographic perspective'. *Journal of Social Issues*, 35, 170–181.

Goldman, R.K. and King, M.J. (1985) 'Counseling Children of Divorce'. *School Psychology Review*, 14, 280–290.

Grollman, E.A. and Grollman, S.H. (1977) 'How to Tell Children About Divorce'. *Journal of Clinical Psychology*, Summer, 35–38.

Guerney, L. and Jordan, K. (1979) 'Children of divorce: A community support group'. *Journal of Divorce*, 2, 283–294.

Hammond, J. (1979) 'Children of divorce: A study of self-concept, academic achievement and values'. *Elementary School Journal*, 80, 55–62.

Henderson, A.J. (1981) 'Designing school guidance programs for single-parent families'. *The School Counselor*, 29, 124–132.

Hess, R.D. and Camara, K.A. (1979) 'Post-divorce family relationships as mediating factors in the consequences of divorce for children'. *Journal of Social Issues*, 35, 79–96.

Hetherington, E.M., Cox, M. and Cox R. (1978) 'The aftermath of divorce'. In J.H. Stevens and M. Mathews (eds.) *Mother/Child Father/Child Relationships*. Washington D.C.: National Association for the Education of Young Children.

Hozman, T.L. and Froiland, D.J. (1976) 'Families in divorce: A proposed model for counseling the children'. *Family Co-Ordinator*, 25(3) 271–275.

Huxley, L. (1963) *You Are Not the Target*. New York: Farrar, Strauss and Giroux, Inc.

Jacobson, G. F. (1983) *The Multiple Crises of Marital Separation and Divorce*. New York: Grune and Stratton.

Janis, J. (1958) *Psychological Stress*. New York: John Wiley and Son.

Kalter, N., Pikar, J. and Lesowitz, M. (1984) 'School-based developmental facilitation groups for children of divorce: A preventive intervention'. *American Journal of Orthopsychiatry*, 54(4).

Koeppen, A.S. (1974) 'Relaxation training for children'. *Elementary School Guidance Counseling*, 9, 14–21.

Kubler-Ross, E. (1969) *On Death and Dying*. New York: MacMillan Publishing Co. Inc.

Larrabee, M.J. and Terres, C.K. (1984) 'Groups: The future of school counseling'. *The School Counselor*, 256–263.

Larrabee, M.J. and Wilson, B.D. (1981) 'Teaching teenagers to cope through family life simulations'. *The School Counselor*, 29, 117–123.

Lazarus, A. (1976) *Multimodal Behaviour Therapy*. New York: Springer.

Lazarus, A.A. (1981) *The Practice of Multimodal Therapy*. New York: McGraw-Hill.

Levine, J. (1977) 'Humor as a Form'. In A.J. Chapman and H.C. Foot (eds.) *It's a Funny Thing, Humour*. International Conference on Humour and Laughter. Welsh Branch, British Psychological Society. Oxford: Pergamon Press.

Lewis, H.W. (1984) 'A structured group counseling program for reading disabled elementary students'. *The School Counselor*, 32(4) 454–459.

Magid, K. (1977) 'Children facing divorce: A treatment program'. *Personnel and Guidance Journal*, 55, 534–536.

Magrab, P.R. (1978) 'For the sake of the children: A review of the psychological effects of divorce'. *Journal of Divorce*, 1, 233–245.

Marris, P. (1978) *Loss and Change*. New York: Anchor Books.

Martin, F.M., Fox, S.J. and Murray, K. (1981) *Children Out of Court*. Edinburgh: Scottish Academic Press.

Maslow, A. (1962) *Toward a Psychology of Being*. Princeton: Van Nostrand.

McDermott, J.F. (1970) 'Divorce and its psychiatric sequalae in children'. *Archives of General Psychiatry*, 23, 421–427.

Meichenbaum, D. and Jaremko, M. (eds.) (1983) *Stress Reduction and Prevention*. New York: Plenum.

Mitchell, A. (1981) *Someone to Turn To: Experiences of Help Before Divorce*. Aberdeen: Aberdeen University Press.

Mitchell, A. (1985) *Children in the Middle: Living Through Divorce*. London and New York: Tavistock Publications.

Novaco, R.W. (1975) *Anger Control: The Development and Evaluation of an Experimental Treatment*. Lexington, MA: Lexington Books.

Raths, L., Harmin, M. and Simon, B. (1978) *Values and Teaching*. Columbus: Charles E. Merrill.

Richards, M.P. and Dyson, M. (1982) *Separation, Divorce and the Development of Children: A Review*. Cambridge: Child Care and Development Group.

Rose, S. (1986) 'Enhancing the Social Relationship Skills of Children'. *School Social Work Journal*, 10, 76–83.

Santrock, J.W. (1972) 'Relation of type and onset of father absence to cognitive development'. *Child Development*, 43, 455–469.

Siepker, B.B. and Kandara, C.S. (eds.) (1985) *Group Therapy with Children and Adolescents: A Treatment Manual*. New York: Human Sciences Press.

Steinmetz, S.K. (1977) *The Cycle of Violence: Assertive, Aggressive and Abusive Family Interaction*. New York: Prager.

Stolberg, A.L. and Anker, J.M. (1984) 'Cognitive and behavioural changes in children resulting from parental divorce and consequent environmental changes'. *Journal of Divorce*, 7, 23–41.

Stolberg, G.A. and Garrison, K.M. (1985) 'Evaluating a primary prevention program for children of divorce'. *American Journal of Community Psychology*, 13(2) 111–124.

Wade, L. (1984) 'A structured group counseling program for reading disabled elementary students'. *The School Counselor*, 454–459.

Wallerstein, J.S. and Bundy, M.L. (1984) 'Helping children of disrupted families: An interview with Judith S. Wallerstein'. *Elementary School Guidance and Counseling*, 19, 19–29.

Whitehead, L. (1979) 'Sex differences in children's responses to family stress: A re-evaluation'. *Journal of Child Psychology and Psychiatry and Allied Disciplines*, 20, 247–254.

Widra, J.M. and Amidon, E. (1987) 'Improving self-concept through intimacy group training'. *Small Group Behaviour*, 18, 269–279.

Wilkinson, G.S. and Bleck, R.T. (1977) 'Children's divorce groups'. *Elementary School Guidance and Counseling*, 2, 205–213.